DEATH IN MUMBAI

A TRUE STORY

MEENAL BAGHEL

PENGUIN BOOKS
An imprint of Penguin Random House

PENGUIN BOOKS

USA | Canada | UK | Ireland | Australia
New Zealand | India | South Africa | China | Singapore

Penguin Books is part of the Penguin Random House group of companies whose addresses can be found at global.penguinrandomhouse.com

Published by Penguin Random House India Pvt. Ltd
4th Floor, Capital Tower 1, MG Road,
Gurugram 122 002, Haryana, India

Penguin Random House India

First published in Random House India in 2011
This edition published in Penguin Books by Penguin Random House India 2019

10 9 8 7 6 5 4 3 2

ISBN 9788184000658

Typeset in Adobe Jenson Pro by SÜRYA, New Delhi
Printed at Repro India Limited

www.penguin.co.in

FSC www.fsc.org MIX Paper from responsible sources FSC® C047271

This is a legitimate digitally printed version of the book and therefore might not have certain extra finishing on the cover.

For my parents, Manjula and Kumar Singh

'Every journalist who is not too stupid or too full of himself to notice what is going on knows that what he does is morally indefensible.'

—Janet Malcolm in *The Journalist and the Murderer*

Contents

Cast of Characters

Neeraj Grover: Television executive from Kanpur who was killed on May 7, 2008 in the apartment of his lover, a Kannada film actress called Maria Susairaj.

Maria Susairaj: Kannada starlet and aspiring television actress. Neeraj Grover was killed and dismembered in her flat in Malad, a Mumbai suburb. She has since been convicted by a Mumbai civil and sessions court for destruction of evidence, and has appealed for exoneration in a higher court.

Emile Jerome: Emile was a naval lieutenant, and Maria's boyfriend, when he killed Neeraj Grover in Maria's apartment. He was convicted of culpable homicide not amounting to murder by the same sessions court, and has since appealed against the decision in the Bombay High Court.

Amarnath Grover: Neeraj Grover's father. He owned a photocopying shop in Kanpur, and now devotes his energies to pursuing justice for his son.

Neelam Grover: Neeraj's mother.

Nishant Lal: A television writer-producer, and one of Neeraj's closest friends in Mumbai. He was a key prosecution witness.

Deepak Kumar: Also works in the television industry. Neeraj's friend and chief troubleshooter in matters of the heart.

Haresh Sondarva: Neeraj's flatmate, who worked in the apparel industry. Haresh left Mumbai after Neeraj's killing.

Sushant Singh: Neeraj's flatmate. He came from Chandigarh to Mumbai to make his mark in Bollywood as a music director.

Deepak Singh: Choreographer and Maria Susairaj's friend. She was his houseguest when she came to Mumbai from Bangalore in April 2008, a few days before Neeraj's death.

Kiran Shreyans: Dance instructor. Maria was acquainted with Kiran in Bangalore, and borrowed his car to dispose of Neeraj's body parts in the jungles of Manor. He was also a prosecution witness in the trial at the city civil and sessions court.

Pavan (His name has been altered upon request): Dance instructor and Maria's former boyfriend.

Richard Susairaj: Maria's brother. Works at their father's construction firm in Bangalore.

Jitesh Saini and Vasanth Kumar: Naval officers and Emile Jerome's friends and course mates. Vasanth, who was

Emile's roommate at the naval base at Kochi, was also a prosecution witness.

Ekta Kapoor: India's most successful television producer, and an astute observer of social mores. Neeraj had worked at her company Balaji Telefilms, and while he was there he met Maria Susairaj and promised her a role in the Balaji serial *Mahabharat*.

Moon Das: A television and stage dancer who aspired to work as an item girl in a big-budget Bollywood film. She was approached to play the role of Maria Susairaj in a movie that was eventually abandoned. Her life was indelibly marked by tragedy when an overly possessive boyfriend went on a shooting spree, in which he killed Moon's mother and uncle.

Ram Gopal Varma: Maverick filmmaker who has directed a film 'inspired' by the Neeraj Grover killing, called *Not a Love Story*.

Rakesh Maria: He was the Joint Commissioner of the Mumbai Crime Branch when Neeraj's father approached him to help trace his son, who seemed to have disappeared overnight. The Crime Branch, along with the local police, finally solved the mystery of Neeraj Grover's death. Rakesh Maria has since moved out of the Crime Branch, and at present heads the Maharashtra Anti-Terrorism Squad.

Inspector Satish Raorane: The chief investigating officer in the case. He is now attached to a police station in Mumbai.

Preface

In the second week of May 2008, the inside pages of the Mumbai newspapers reported the story of a twenty-five-year-old television executive from Kanpur who had gone missing. He was last seen on May 6 at the suburban home of his lover, a little-known Kannada film actress named Maria Monica Susairaj.

The story moved to the front page two weeks later, when Rakesh Maria, the savvy boss of the Mumbai Crime Branch, held a press conference in which he announced that the missing television executive, Neeraj Grover, was dead. It was, the officer enunciated with customary deliberation, allowing the scribes to take down each word, the case of a love triangle gone horribly wrong. Neeraj Grover, he alleged, had been killed by Maria Susairaj, aged twenty-eight, and her naval officer fiancé Lieutenant Emile Jerome, aged twenty-five. After killing Neeraj the couple had cut his body up into 'several bits', and disposed of it in the jungles of Manor, a picnic spot on the outskirts of Mumbai.

The story could not have been more dramatic had it been scripted. It had all the key ingredients for a media frenzy—young, beautiful, ambitious people involved in a gruesome killing. It became the year's biggest crime story, with each emerging detail lapped up by an avid audience. The press outdid each other with wild speculations. When one young reporter at a leading television channel called up his bosses in Delhi to alert them to the news, they didn't ask him about the who, what, when, where, why, and how—those classic cornerstones of reporting—but a more Gabbar-like question: 'Kitne tukde the?' (How many pieces were there?)

When the reporter, quoting Rakesh Maria, responded with 'several bits', the television bosses added three and three and came up with three hundred. 'If a chicken can be cut into ten, twelve pieces, it follows that a five foot eleven inch man would be cut into three hundred pieces,' they insisted before running the headline.

The effect of this revelation was sensational. The killing suddenly seemed more vivid; the criminals more monstrous. Neeraj had not simply been killed. He had been hacked into three hundred pieces. As Neeraj's distraught mother Neelam Grover said when I first spoke to her on the phone: 'Just see how they cut up my son, that's not the work of ordinary folks but evil sorcerers.' They were 'chudail, pishach', she said, 'not human beings'.

Killing is rarely a sophisticated act. It arises out of too many unbridled passions—anger, greed, jealousy, lust. Here were three people blessed with many favours through their lives—they were young, educated, each talented in their own way, beautiful, and from comfortable middle class backgrounds. What dark undercurrents in their personalities drew them to one another? What really transpired through the night of May 6 and 7 that led them to lose control, and erase the possibilities that life offered?

Several comparisons have been drawn between this case and the famous Nanavati murder case of 1959, in which a naval officer, Kawas Nanavati, killed his English wife's lover, a wealthy Mumbai businessman called Prem Ahuja. Nanavati, having learnt of his wife's infidelity, confronted Ahuja about the affair as he lay in his bathtub, eliciting the response, 'Am I supposed to marry every woman I sleep with?'

Similarly, Lieutenant Emile Jerome rushed from Kochi to Mumbai when he found out that Neeraj Grover was at his girlfriend's house late on the night of May 6. He arrived at Maria's door early in the morning, and went straight into her bedroom to verify his suspicions. Neeraj Grover, allegedly lying in a state of dishabille, opened his eyes and looked at Emile, then at Maria: 'Oh, so this is the fiancé?' he remarked.

Grover's and Ahuja's impulse to provoke may have been the same, but what followed is what separates the two cases entirely. After shooting Ahuja dead, a repentant Nanavati immediately went to the police and surrendered. Emile and Maria allegedly dismembered Neeraj's body for quick disposal, and for two weeks thereafter behaved as if nothing was amiss. They exhibited none of the remorse that follows a temporary loss of control—the guilt which lent a certain nobility to Dostoevsky's murderer Raskolnikov.

From the time it broke, the story of the killing of Neeraj Grover was owned by television. Crime, not Bollywood, is our salutary entertainment. We end our days with *Sansani, Vaardaat,* and *Dus Tak,* in the company of hirsute anchors, each noisier than the other. I too came to the story through a visual medium. Late one evening, I walked into the photographers' bay at the office of *Mumbai Mirror,* the newspaper I edit, to see my colleague Raju Shinde produce a series of powerful pictures of Neeraj's parents breaking down upon seeing their son's assailants at the police station.

Their grief-strained faces, and their fight for control, were immensely affecting. But, most of all, as Raju reported, it was Neelam Grover's ringing question to her son's killers—'Why? Why did you kill Neeraj?'—that arrested attention. There has been no answer.

MEENAL BAGHEL
July 2011, Mumbai

Book I

The Journey: From Mysore to Mumbai

1

THE KILLING

'You, lady, are my number one suspect.'

—Rakesh Maria, Head of the Mumbai Crime Branch,
to Maria Susairaj

THE HEART OF Oshiwara lies on land reclaimed from slushy backwaters in the late seventies. Large swathes of Mumbai have been 'reclaimed', as if the sea were an encroacher against whom a case had been filed and won. When Ekta Kapoor moved here in 2000 to set up Balaji Telefilms, Oshiwara was in her words, a 'dump'. 'I was quite horrified at having landed in such a rotten place. All you ever saw were arty-type people with big bindis.' Television's most famous backroom girl wears her hair stylishly cut, and is dressed on a working day in a tracksuit. It hints as much to her get-up-and-go attitude, as it does to her preoccupation with her weight.

In the decade since Ekta's arrival, this North Mumbai district has become the nerve centre of the entertainment industry, renewing Mumbai's sagging energy after most of its manufacturing industries moved to other parts of India, offering cheaper real estate and investor-friendly policies.

In reality, the nation's popular culture filtered out from just one unremarkable, potholed back alley of the Shah Industrial Estate, where Balaji Telefilms and the Yash Raj Films (YRF) studios stand at right angles, surrounded by a foundry, a derelict warehouse, and an unkempt ground that is hired out for receptions during the wedding season. While the snooty guards at YRF shoo away aspiring stars for daydreaming at its impenetrable gates, Balaji, in keeping with the more democratic nature of its medium, has a notice at the door that spells hope: 'Leave two photographs with the watchman, if we like them we will get back in two days.'

Aside from the shiny, glass-fronted buildings that have mushroomed on the marshes, there has also been a sartorial sea change from those big bindi days that so horrified Ekta. Now the neighbourhood was full of mini-skirted brides flaunting their choodas along with their stilettos, and men in distressed jeans and sleeveless ganjis baring bench-press biceps and showing off fake tattoos. In India's capital of make-believe, even rebellion is a 'look'.

On a sullen, clammy April evening in 2008, television executive Deepak Kumar was sitting at the coffee shop at Fun Republic, a one-stop entertainment centre, a few yards away from these dream factories. He sprawled into a steel and rattan chair and ran a hand over his buzz-cut as he discreetly observed the ladies. He was waiting for the rest of his gang to arrive. The 'Coffee House Nomads', as the group called itself, met at this Café Coffee Day each evening after work. The waiter knew their preferences, and the café offered them a chance to sit under the open sky, escape the dingy sets and frigid editing suites. Here, they could pretend that the great Mumbai obsession, 'time pass', was a legitimate pursuit.

Deepak Kumar and his closest friends, Nishant Lal and Neeraj Grover, were in their twenties and had come to Mumbai within a few years of each other, united in their ambition to work in television. They had a common link to Delhi—they shared its Hindi heartland sensibilities, and also a camaraderie that is particular to young bachelors.

Deepak Kumar worked with a television production house, Shreya Creations, steadily rising to become an executive producer. Neeraj, the lean and hungry hop-skip-jump man, had just quit Balaji Telefilms and joined Cinevista as creative producer, but was already in talks with Synergie Adlabs; while Nishant, the long-haired leader of their group, was his own boss, conceptualizing shows for different channels.

Neeraj had been the last to join the Coffee House Nomads, a year ago, in 2007. He had stood out in the Fun Republic foyer for his good looks, talking up a storm as he paced around the flyweight tables, nervously transferring an unlit cigarette from his fingers to his lips and back, making loud references to working with Amitabh Bachchan, for whoever cared to listen.

Nishant, blowing smoke rings in the air, his large, gentle eyes missing nothing, had watched the boy with amusement. Neeraj had turned up again the next day, approached their table for a light, and introduced himself.

A Kanpuria!

As they had suspected, Neeraj had landed in Mumbai just a few months ago. He was working on a Kannada ad film for Dabur with the superstar. The three young men got talking. Neeraj turned out to be a jolly, witty boy who got all the jokes. Nishant, who had been working on a show called *Aaghaz,* urgently needed an actor for a day and Neeraj, with his clean-cut good looks and lean frame, fit the bill. The three began to hang out after the shoot, revelling in the warm flush of sudden and deep friendship. No topic was exempt from their boisterous discussions: movies, sport, cars, bikes, Vijay Mallya (whose lifestyle they aspired to), parents, friends, travel, gizmos, and—with Neeraj around—inevitably, women.

With the awe that is characteristic of ordinary monogamous mortals, Deepak Kumar watched a succession of young women sashay into their lives, offering him vague, glassy-eyed hellos before transforming into animated, honeydew goddesses around Neeraj. 'Mere hisse ki ladkiyan bhi tumhare hisse mein rehti hain!' (Your lot includes my share of women too), the thickset young man often grumbled good-naturedly, by now resigned to taking vicarious pleasure in his friend's amorous triumphs. Though sometimes these could get him into trouble. Neeraj had recently violated the sacred code—don't dip your nib in the office ink—by getting involved with a young woman who worked with him at Balaji, and who was a part of their gang. When he turned his charms on her and presented her with a bauble as a 'pretend' engagement ring, she hadn't been able to resist his proposal, risking her relationship with her steady boyfriend.

When Neeraj got bored after a couple of months and moved on, the jilted woman, sullen, hurt and angry, had blamed Deepak for not warning her about the new girl. But he really hadn't known. Neeraj made his moves faster than Vishwanathan Anand did playing speed chess.

For the last few days, Neeraj had been talking about an actress from Bangalore called Maria Susairaj. He had helped her audition for Balaji's big upcoming show, *Mahabharat,* that March. The two had met earlier in 2007 and had recognized the spark of attraction between them—but before it could blossom into something deeper, Maria had shifted back to Bangalore to work on a Kannada film, *Ekdant*. After they reconnected for the *Mahabharat* audition, they kept in touch regularly over the phone. Maria, Neeraj told his friends, was coming back to Mumbai in the last week of April, and today's coffee house discussion was devoted to Neeraj's opening gambit.

Nirvana lies less than a kilometre away from Fun Republic, past the offices of film producers and big movie posters that dwarf the sky; between a police station so small that cars confiscated from criminals have to be parked illegally on the road, and a petrol pump modelled on Delhi's Baha'i

Lotus Temple. The soot, the exhaust fumes, and the film of fuel have left the petrol pump looking like an overripe cabbage instead.

Beautiful, skinny, young white women limber across the dirty open corridor that leads to the dance rehearsal hall like welcoming apsaras, oblivious to the April heat, pirouetting, pouting, and arching a leg in the air while the peon from the next door office passes by without a second glance.

Behind thick, soundproof walls lay Nirvana, a hall where auditions for Bollywood films and reality TV shows were held. Inside, the air conditioner was on full blast, and the music system blared '*Mauja hi Mauja*'. '1-2, 1-2 Kick! 1-2, 1-2 Kick!' A young choreographer instructed like a drill sergeant shaking her head—the Caucasians didn't get it. They danced stiffly, using their shoulders—the Indian girls danced with their hips, much more sensually; but they weren't white-skinned.

From the corner of the room, senior choreographer Deepak Singh raised a placatory hand, a small frown marring the repose of his comic-book Buddha face. He stretched his lithe, sweat-slickened body and instructed his assistant, the young drill sergeant choreographer, to organize another batch of Russian and Ukrainian girls for auditions the next day.

The day was not going well for Deepak. It had begun with a rather unsettling call from Maria Monica Susairaj. She was the ex-girlfriend of a friend from Bangalore, Pavan. They had all known each other at a dance training school that Pavan ran called Studio 5678. The actress, known as Maria in Mumbai, but always as Monica to friends and intimates back home in Mysore and Bangalore, had called to announce that she was arriving in Mumbai on April 29 to give acting one final shot. She asked if she could stay with Deepak Singh for the next few days, until she found her own place. The choreographer was taken aback by the directness of her request, but she had been sweetly persistent. 'Just for a few days. . . Please, please. I'll find another place soon. My dad is willing to give me the down payment for a flat. Help me out this one time.'

There was something disquieting about Maria's constant flitting from city to city, from one ambition to another. She and Deepak had met in Mumbai just a month ago, in March 2008, when she told him about her engagement to a naval officer. They had gone to the Lokhandwala market together to buy some shirts for her fiancé. 'I am finally ready to settle down,' she had said. If she was marrying in a few months and shifting to a naval base, why did she want to move into a new flat, and, why after the many disappointments, when none of her previous visits yielded that elusive film role, did she want to chance her luck again in Mumbai? Deepak Singh ran his hand through his limp ponytail, towelled himself dry, and moved decisively towards the exit of the dance hall. What Maria Monica did with her life was none of his business; nor did he particularly care. After the success of two televisions shows, his own life was on the up, and he was on his way to becoming a known choreographer, something he and his friends had only dreamed of back in Bangalore. He would offer her his hospitality for a few days, for old times' sake. It was what you did when someone from Studio 5678 moved to strike it big in Mumbai.

In private, friends often jestingly likened Neeraj to a 'C-grade' Casanova. He could be indiscriminate, trying for every girl, with his silly jokes: 'Jo hansi, woh phansi' (If she falls for your jokes, she falls for you). Even so, when his friends finally met Maria at their Café Coffee Day adda, they were surprised at what they saw. She was mousy, with pronounced dark circles under her eyes, and looked much older than Neeraj's twenty-five years. She hardly spoke, and when she did, she was soft-spoken to the point of being inaudible. She seemed vulnerable, and not like the tough television girls that were Neeraj's staple. She told them she had studied engineering in Mysore, then mentioned 'a diploma in interior design', amending it to say, 'No, actually, I have studied dance.'

Nishant Lal was already bored.

After she left Café Coffee Day, Neeraj's friend ribbed him, tickled that Maria had auditioned for no less than Draupadi's role in *Mahabharat*. 'She's a modern chick. She speaks in SMSs, 120 characters and no more. Ha, ha!' And so on, the sophomoric jokes continued.

Neeraj smiled, ignoring them. 'Hum logon ke beech mein sab kuch hota hai,' he told them as if nothing else was relevant.

Maria Susairaj had landed in Mumbai on April 29, 2008, and reconnected with Neeraj. He had organized a couple of auditions for her and they immediately fell into a relationship, as if fast-forwarding an old spark to its logical end.

Neeraj did seem quite taken with Maria, Nishant observed. Soon after Maria's arrival in Mumbai he stopped hanging out with his friends, preferring to spend all his time with her. At night, instead of dropping her off at her choreographer friend Deepak Singh's house in Borivali he took her to his two-bedroom flat in Andheri, which he shared with his cousin and friends—Haresh, Sushant, and Sushant's wife and children.

It was well past midnight when Neeraj's roommate, Haresh Sondarva, was woken from his deep slumber. It was Neeraj, with that guilty entreaty that Haresh had come to dread.

'Not again!'

'Please yaar. Please, she's waiting outside.'

Without another word Haresh rolled his lean frame out of his bed. A petite girl waited in the darkened room outside. They exchanged hellos in theatrical whispers. Neeraj, after backslapping his thanks, guided her into the bedroom. After half an hour of sleeplessness and staring at the dark ceiling, Haresh plumped the pillow, tossing about like a fish thrashing on the beach, and resolved to speak to Neeraj and the others in the house the next morning.

Haresh had moved to Mumbai in October 2006 after receiving his diploma in fashion design from NIFT, Gandhinagar, and short stints in Pune and Delhi, to join that lowest species of Mumbai's single male populace—the sub-subletter. An aspiring filmmaker had been the original tenant of the spacious two-bedroom flat at Jyoti Apartments, Seven Bungalows, Andheri. He had taken in Haresh's friend as a subletter, who in turn had invited Haresh to rent from him. A flat by the sea, he had been told. While you couldn't quite see the sea you could smell the fish, so Haresh couldn't quibble about semantics.

When Neeraj started living with them three months later, Haresh was happy, imagining that he had moved up a notch in the tenant hierarchy. Besides, he liked Neeraj. They were the two smokers in the flat, and both shared pleasant memories of haunting Delhi's Saket Market.

When Haresh's friend and the filmmaker moved out after a few months, he and Neeraj took over the lease. But Neeraj's stream of girlfriends had not gone unnoticed. There were mutterings from members of the housing society about the goings-on at A-10. That's when Sushant, an aspiring music director from Chandigarh, was roped in. Sushant's biggest qualification was that he was married. The lease was redrawn in his name, giving him automatic access to one of the two bedrooms, leaving Neeraj and Haresh to share the other.

Sushant, at thirty-five, the oldest among them by several years, brought with him the baggage of marriage and domesticity. The bare bachelors' pad was soon furnished. He bought a fridge, stocked it with juices, fruit, vegetables, and cooked food, and insisted that they all eat at least one meal together. Months later, when his wife and their two children moved in, the house lost all the vestiges of a bachelors' pad. The morning after Haresh was rudely awoken, Sushant's wife put her foot down. 'I don't like this girl's vibe,' she informed them.

Neeraj pleaded with his flatmates to let Maria stay on for a few days until she got her own place. 'She has no place to go to, I am helping her find a house.' Haresh found himself caught between guilt for complaining, and embarrassment at the broadsides directed at Maria by the others—until he found an ATM slip lying on top of Maria's handbag, and against his better judgement picked it up. Her bank account showed a deposit of Rs 55,000. If she had so much money, he wondered, why did she not stay in a hotel and save herself the humiliation?

Maria's choreographer friend Deepak Singh had also taken note of the mysterious movements of his houseguest. Not because he was troubled by her—on the contrary, she had been an impeccable guest.

Other than the three or four pieces of luggage that had been neatly stacked in one room, there was little evidence of her in his apartment. He had been prepared for forced conviviality, for long, boring reminiscences about their Bangalore days, but Maria was a fleeting presence. She stayed out the entire day—house hunting, she told him—only to return in the evenings to freshen up and go out again at night.

'Where do you go every evening?' he was curious to know.

'To Café Coffee Day at Fun Republic with Neeraj,' she replied matter-of-factly, looking him straight in the eye. He didn't ask her about the nights, and she didn't volunteer information. He did wonder about this new man Neeraj, and where that left her fiancé the naval officer, but once again, he restrained himself. It wasn't his place to probe. It sufficed that when he woke up in the mornings she was returning home.

With great attentiveness she would make him coffee and breakfast, and they would stand leisurely around the kitchen, yakking in Tamil instead of the Kannada they spoke with their other friends. She could be a comforting presence, and he wouldn't have minded if she were around more often, Deepak Singh thought, surprising himself.

So that evening when he bumped into an old Bangalore friend who was passing through Mumbai, Deepak decided to host an impromptu party. He also invited another old Studio 5678 mate, Kiran Shreyans. When Maria returned from house hunting he asked her to stay. 'You go out every evening. . . Everyone is coming here, and we'll all be meeting after a long time. Why not stay at home tonight? Let's have a party.'

When Kiran, who now worked in Andheri as a dance instructor, walked in, he briefly lost his smile, surprised to see Maria. But the flash in his large dramatic eyes was quickly banked. When Maria had come to Mumbai in 2005 to try her luck in films, she had been friends with the curly-haired young man and his girlfriend; but Maria, whom Kiran was to later call 'shrewd and manipulative', had created problems between the couple, leading to a bitter break-up. Kiran had not forgiven Maria for it, but for that evening the vivacity and the warmth of his other friends dispelled all unpleasantness.

Soon, the Bangalore gang was carousing happily. One of the girls sang, her beautiful voice soaring through the quiet night, with Maria's more mellow but sonorous voice joining in. They ate copious amounts of food, they laughed, sang their old favourite, 'Moongda'. Then, drunk on spirit and happy memories, the old friends danced around Deepak's living room, crashing out in the early hours like dorm-mates, oblivious to the upheaval snaking around the corner.

Maria knew her audition for the role of Draupadi had not gone well—all those Sanskritized dialogues: '*Upasthit samast gurujan, aaj Hastinapur mein mera apmaan hua hai. Draupadi jo Panchal naresh ki putri hai*' (Elders, teachers, Draupadi, daughter of the ruler of Panchal, has been humiliated in your august presence in Hastinapur today), etc., etc., were a mouthful. Her old friend, the actor-director Sachin Pilgaonkar, had been recommending a diction class, but Neeraj had been sanguine.

Balaji Telefilms had tied up with the now-defunct baaja.com for a talent hunt, where aspirants were invited to post their pictures on the site. Maria, who had sent in her photographs, wrote obsessively on the site enquiring after a response. But she did not hear back from them.

Later, when he joined Synergie Adlabs, Neeraj got her an audition for one of the shows Synergie was producing, but nothing came of that either. Jaldi hi something will work out, he said, stalling her persistent queries. His promises to get her work soon were so baroque that she began to wonder if he took her seriously at all.

Another visit, this time to actress-turned-producer Aruna Irani's office, also yielded nothing. They had taken her portfolio pictures, looked at them cursorily, and then tossed them aside without even the pretence of politeness. When she told Neeraj's friend Nishant Lal about her disheartening day, he asked to see her portfolio. There were pictures of a plain girl, plainly shot, that would get her nowhere. The photographs were a stark reminder of the difference between Bangalore's fledgling glamour and Mumbai's airbrushed world.

'Don't you have any others?'

'None with me right now but there are some on Orkut.'

She logged in on her laptop and showed him photographs of her family, her younger sister whom she was closest to in the family, her Mysore and Bangalore friends, and some solo snapshots from her days as a Kannada film actress.

'This one,' he tapped the monitor. It was the picture of a younger, fuller Maria, with a different, more flattering hairstyle, and an alluring smile. It hinted at a confident beauty, a far cry from the shrunken, hollow-eyed girl in front of him.

'This is the picture you must circulate.'

Two days later Neeraj was at Café Coffee Day with the Nomads when Maria came over to their table, her angry flounce an indication of which way the conversation was going to go. She drew Neeraj to one side to speak to him in private. Girl trouble, sniggered his friends, and when he returned to the table Neeraj looked downcast. At 11.45 pm, he called Nishant Lal, who was having dinner with his girlfriend at Zafran, a restaurant in Oshiwara, wanting to discuss the Maria problem.

'What's the stress about?' asked Nishant.

Maria had realized that Neeraj did not have the clout to get her roles, and now she also doubted his romantic intentions. Following another altercation she had gone off to a pub, Firangi Paani, to drink by herself, expecting that Neeraj would follow. They had also bickered over his flatmates' refusal to let her stay with him. 'We've finalized a house for her in Malad, it's a matter of a couple of days,' he said, asking Nishant if he and Maria could come over to his flat and spend a night.

Despite their disagreements, it was understood that Maria would spend the nights with Neeraj. When they came to Zafran to pick up the keys to his flat, Nishant noticed her swollen eyes and the tension sitting thickly between the young couple.

The evening was pleasant with a drowsy breeze, and when Nishant got back home the lights in the house were dim. He went to his room, leaving Neeraj and Maria alone and switched on the radio. Almost as if in keeping with the sombre mood, one of his favourite songs came on air, '*Raat hamari to chand ki saheli hai, kitne dinon ke baad, aayi woh akeli hai...*' (The night is a friend of the moon, but after a long while she has stepped out alone...) from the film *Parineeta*. As he sat back, a sweetly piercing voice joined in from the other room. He had no idea Maria had such a beautiful voice. He switched off the radio and leaned against the door looking into the room where she sat with Neeraj. '*Andhera rootha hai, gumsum sa kone main baitha hai. . .*' (The darkness sulks in a corner. . .). She sang with great poignancy and Nishant, looking at her, her beauty protean in the lamp light, her voice deeply affecting, found himself involuntarily drawn to this slight girl. In the silence after the song ended he cleared his throat, asking for an encore.

Later, drawing Nishant aside, she asked, abruptly demanding an answer: 'Is Neeraj cheating on me?' He stared down at her, his face impassive. 'That only he can answer. Good night, Maria.'

Whenever the Coffee House Nomads had spare cash they shifted their venue, and changed their beverage of choice. D'Ultimate, a neon and steel discotheque built inside an industrial warehouse, just a lane away from Fun Republic, was perfect for their purposes. If they pooled in there was enough money to get good booze and the disc jockey played just the right mix of English music and Bollywood chartbusters. In the darkness, nearly swallowed up by the black leather sofa, Nishant saw that all their friends had made it to the party. Neeraj and Maria walked in past midnight, hand in hand, and began dancing closely with one another. They kissed passionately, their body language advertising their intimacy. Maria seemed happy and unusually talkative. 'I've never seen such a close-knit bunch—you guys are great, and Neeraj is lucky to have such friends,' she told Nishant, and then, just as he thought all her issues with Neeraj were over, she drew closer to him and Deepak Kumar and asked with an urgency in her voice, 'Can Neeraj be trusted? He won't let me down, will he?'

May 6, 2008, 8 am, Deepak Singh's apartment

Deepak Singh woke up to the sound of something screeching against the floor. Maria was lugging her heavy suitcase across the room.

'Hi, sorry, just trying to load this in the taxi.'

He effortlessly loaded the suitcases one after the other on to the carrier. Maria had found a one-bedroom flat at Malad in Dheeraj Solitaire, the same building where she had stayed during an earlier stint in Mumbai. As promised, she had not overstayed her welcome—even by a day. 'Romba, thanks.'

There was a brief moment of awkwardness between them, dispelled by a quick hug and goodbye. 'You take care, ya, we'll keep in touch.'

Maria got into the taxi, and Deepak watched her go off in the direction of her new home. He didn't know that Maria would be taking a little detour. According to the watchman at Dheeraj Solitaire, Malad, the new tenant in 201-B did not arrive in a taxi, but in a black Scorpio, and neither did she come alone. He remembered because she was accompanied by a movie and television star he had grown up watching on screen. He remembered being impressed.

May 6, 9.30 pm, Neeraj Grover's apartment

Sushant Singh looked happily around the well-laden dinner table. Seated around him were his wife, his children, Haresh, Neeraj's cousin, and an empty chair for Neeraj who was washing up before joining them. It was one of those rare days when all of them got together for a meal. Sushant missed the big family dinners in Chandigarh when the entire family would sit around and share the travails of the day, or laugh and talk until long after the food had dried on their fingers. Mumbai, it gave you many things, par chain ka khaana nahin. He was also happy that the embarrassing Maria chapter was behind them. Neeraj had told them that she had moved into her own flat this morning. He seemed to have forgotten the brief unpleasantness between them all. When Neeraj's phone, which was kept on the table, rang persistently, he peered over to check the number and raised his eyebrows.

'Maria.'

She wanted Neeraj to come over to her flat. 'Not tonight, I have an early morning meeting, I'll stay at home,' Neeraj told her and settled down to dinner. At 9.55 pm the phone rang again. 'Babe, really, let it be, I've just started my dinner. . .'

After a long pause in which he did most of the listening, Neeraj scraped back his chair, smiling apologetically. 'She's calling me, I have to go.'

'At least finish your food,' Sushant remonstrated.

'Paaji,' he snapped his fingers, his goofy grin betraying his lie, 'Main bas abhi gaya, aur abhi aaya' (I'll be back in a jiffy).

May 7, 7.30 am, Maria's new apartment

Kundan Jha, the watchman at Dheeraj Solitaire, rubbed his sleepy eyes and pushed the register forward for the handsome young man to make his entry. Jha neither understood nor read English. The visitor could have entered any gibberish, but it was protocol, and if there was one thing Kundan Jha had learnt in Mumbai, it was that here, unlike back home in Nawada, Bihar, rules must be followed.

The new memsahib in 201-B seemed popular. She had arrived the previous morning with an actor, then last night another young man had arrived and not left since, followed by the delivery man from Sai Sagar restaurant a little after 11 pm—and now the day had just started, and here was another visitor carrying a backpack and refusing to write his name.

'I am a cousin,' he said moving away.

'Par naam kya hai?' Kundan Jha said, insisting that he reveal his name.

Back home in Bihar the women of his house led strictly circumscribed lives. In Mumbai, Kundan Jha saw a different breed of woman and didn't bat an eyelid, relishing his own insouciance. This is what the big city was all about—being modern.

Emile Jerome never did make that entry; the first of his many moves that confused the prosecution later.

May 7, 1 pm, the home of Kiran Shreyans

Kiran Shreyans, on the other hand, was petrified by this modernity. After a messy break-up with his long-time girlfriend, the one he had moved from Bangalore to Mumbai for, he was no longer sure of how to deal with women. The rules of the man–woman relationship he had grown up observing had been subverted. As the good-looking dance instructor at Andheri's Renaissance Federation Board Club, he was surrounded by beautiful, willing women. Sex was available on call, but not emotional succour. As if merely thinking of difficult modern women could conjure up a presence, his phone rang. It was Maria Susairaj.

Despite the enjoyable evening at their mutual friend Deepak Singh's house four days ago, Kiran had retained his misgivings about Maria. Her soft voice was unnaturally shrill, and he couldn't quite pinpoint if she sounded anxious or just overeager.

'Kiran, could I please borrow your car for a bit? My fiancé has come from Kochi to join the naval base in Mumbai, and he has lots of luggage. I just need to drop him to Colaba, after which I'll return your car.'

Kiran paused wordlessly; it was the best way he knew how to say no. 'Please, Kiran, please, please, please, please, please, please...' she persisted, like a spoilt child who knows she will get her way if she pleads long enough.

'Okay, but I have to go out for dinner tonight, so make sure that you return it by 9–9.30 pm.'

About three hours later Maria and her naval officer boyfriend were at his door.

'Kiran, many thanks, ya. This is Emile, my fiance.'

He misheard the name as ML. What kind of a name was that? But the chap seemed fine. Cool, collected. Instead, Kiran found himself distracted by the many love bites on

Maria's neck and chest. He tried hard not to look, but couldn't help staring at the marks across her chest where the buttons met, and all over her neck.

Evidently, distance was good for some relationships.

They walked to where the car was parked and he handed over his car keys to Maria, sneaking a discreet look at the fuel gauge.

'Be careful with my car and bring it back by the evening.'

It was only after they left that it occurred to him—why plead so hard for his car? Why not take a taxi like the rest of Mumbai?

By ten in the evening there was no sign of Maria, Emile, or the car. When he called her, she sounded distracted, apologetic. 'I am really sorry about the car, Kiran, but one of my friends, Neeraj, has gone missing and we're all so worried. I am at the police station right now and we're lodging a complaint. If possible I'll drop your car later tonight or tomorrow morning.'

Next morning, through his window, Kiran saw Emile drive the Santro into the compound and park it clumsily. Without waiting for them to come up to the house he went out to park it properly. Maria apologized profusely for the delay and tried to push Rs 200 into his hand. For the petrol used, she offered lamely. Kiran laughed her off and checked the fuel gauge; the needle was exactly where it had been when he had given the car to them yesterday. Clearly that had been taken care of.

Three days after they had returned his car, Maria called again with a baffling query. 'Have any cops called you?'

'Why should the police call me?'

'They may call, it could be in connection with my friend's disappearance, the one I told you about, Neeraj,' she sounded tense.

A few days later she called again. 'Did the police call you yet?' This time Kiran noted a distinct trace of hysteria.

'You know the case has been transferred to the Crime Branch and they're tracking it closely, I think they're tapping my number.'

He couldn't help but laugh out loud. Was she suffering from paranoia? 'Don't worry, Monica, the Crime Branch doesn't tap ordinary people's phones. Your friend will soon turn up.'

Barely ten minutes later the phone rang again. It was Maria again, the urgency in her voice unmistakable.

'Kiran, if the police calls you and asks about me, please tell them that I had come to your house to borrow Rs 3,000, which I came and returned the next day. Don't forget, okay? Just say this much and nothing else. Please!'

Kiran disconnected the call and stared at his feet, his heart drumming up a heavy rhythm in his chest, panic swelling like nausea up his throat. He took the car keys off the hook and raced down to the parking lot. He opened the boot of the blue-grey Santro, desperately scanning for telltale signs, not knowing what he was looking for. The stepney, the spanners, everything seemed in place. He looked again carefully, and for long. There was nothing untoward. He shut the boot, and leaned against it to catch his breath. He failed to check the back seat. Had he looked in the crevice between the backrest and the seat, he would have found two discolorations caused by patches of blood drying on the tapestry.

May 7, 10 am, Neeraj Grover's home in Kanpur

Neeraj was not answering his phone. Maybe he'd had a late night and was sleeping it off. Neelam Grover decided she would wait for another half an hour before calling her son again. Ever since Ginni (as they called him at home) had left Kanpur, first to study at Amity University in Noida, and then to work in Mumbai, the mother and son spoke to each other twice a day, every day. Once at around ten in the morning, and then again at eleven in the night.

Amarnath Grover would often ask his wife what was it that transpired through the night that necessitated the morning call; but it was never more than a mock complaint. It was good that Ginni was close to his mother. He, who himself had a slightly more formal relationship with his children, felt comforted by the fact that they had grown up with the right values. His second-born may live away from home but as the calls demonstrated, Ginni was anchored to them.

One day, he hoped, Neeraj would have his fill of the world of glamour and return to Kanpur, like Amarnath Grover himself had done, taking voluntary retirement from his job, to set up a stationery shop on Mall Road. It may not offer the glamour of Neeraj's television world, but that little shop, which had expanded over the years, and his nifty investments, had served the family well.

Half an hour later Neelam Grover dialled her son again. The phone rang, each ring echoing the other. 'I'll wait for exactly ten rings,' she promised herself, and then reluctantly disconnected after the eleventh. She'd spoken to him last night at 11.15 pm after watching *Kayamath*. Though Neeraj had left Balaji, his name still appeared in the credits of their lead show. Every day, she looked for it, and then called him. 'Ginni, they are still running your name as the creative producer.'

He had laughed, sounding happy and in good spirits. Maybe he was in the shower, maybe he was talking to someone in the other room. She called again. Then five minutes later, again. She pressed redial, then superstitiously dialled his entire number. Redial once more. The half-peeled vegetables lay forgotten in the kitchen as she fervently punched the keys on her phone. Again. Again. Again.

She called her daughter to complain. 'Ginni is not taking his calls.'

Separated by only two years, the brother and sister shared a special bond. Maybe he would be persuaded to answer Shikha's call. But as she soon informed her mother, he still wasn't picking up. Shikha next called her cousin who was living with Neeraj in Mumbai. He too had no news. 'Ginni didn't come back home last night and he's not answering any calls either. He's also not at work, what's with him, yaar?' he complained instead.

Before leaving to collect her children from school, Shikha made another quick call to her mother, her fingers crossed behind her back. 'Mummy, Neeraj shoot pe hai. His phone is on silent, you can talk to him at night.'

She kept dialling her brother's number, each unanswered call like a tentacle clamping around her heart. Determined not to worry her parents yet, she called her uncle, Satnam Arora. Her mother's brother was a resourceful man. 'Ginni is not answering his phone, he's not at home, nor at work, and no one in Mumbai seems to know where he is. I haven't yet told mummy, papa.'

Satnam Arora promptly called his business associates in Mumbai and set them to work. 'Tu worry mat kar, he'll be around somewhere, we'll soon find out.'

That day, May 7, 2008, the Grovers called Neeraj one hundred and thirty times. The phone was answered only once. Somewhere between 4 pm and 5 pm when Shikha called, the call connected after the fourth ring.

'Ginni! Hello, Ginni, Can you hear me? Ginni, hello!' But all she heard was a muffled sound, and some voices talking far away.

'Ginni,' she called out urgently. But there was just the fluttering invective of the wind before the phone went dead. This was the call that would eventually unravel the mystery of Neeraj's disappearance.

May 7, around noon, Nishant Lal's home

Nishant Lal was still at home when Maria called to say that Neeraj had left his phone at her house last night. 'He left at 1.30 am to go to your place,' she said.

'But he never turned up here,' Nishant told her. 'In fact I got a call from his office this morning, asking me where he was, he has missed an important meeting.'

'I don't know about that but his phone is here, and he hasn't called for it. Will you please collect it from me either at Café Coffee Day, or from my home, or if you speak to Neeraj, ask him to?'

So he was not with Maria. For the first time since the call from Neeraj's office, Nishant felt concern. Where the bloody hell was Neeraj? He checked with Deepak Kumar who had also not heard from Neeraj, though the friends spoke every day without fail. 'Yeh saala ullu banaa raha hai humein. He's up to some juvenile prank,' said Deepak with uncertainty. 'Let's meet Maria in the evening and find out what games Mr Neeraj Grover is playing.'

May 7, a little after 9 pm, Maria's new apartment

Instead of meeting at Café Coffee Day, Maria had asked Nishant Lal and Deepak Kumar to come over to her flat. 'When you reach Dheeraj Solitaire call me and I'll come down with the phone.' They thought it distinctly odd that she had not invited them upstairs. They had been pacing the foyer for five minutes when she came down with Neeraj's phone. She was dressed smartly and looked freshly scrubbed.

Before she could say anything Deepak butted in. 'Come on, Maria, show us your new flat.' As she baulked, taken aback by their directness, Deepak Kumar called for the elevator, his big bulky frame practically herding them into the small lift. Inside the tiny, skeletal flat, bereft of any furnishing, Deepak parodied Sherlock Holmes. He was convinced Neeraj would emerge grinning any second.

'Hel-llo!' He snuck from the living room into the kitchen, shielding his eyes with his palms in the classic bumbling sleuth pose, before stopping short abruptly at the doorway to the bedroom.

Inside was a bare-chested man fiddling with a laptop. Feeling suddenly foolish Deepak returned to the living room.

'Hey, Emile,' Maria called out.

Instead of Neeraj, a good-looking stranger with a serious demeanour and sooty eyes emerged. 'This is Emile Jerome, my fiancé. He's with the navy, and he's just been posted to Mumbai.'

Deepak and Nishant stared at one another and in that split second, both men reached the same decision.

'Maria, we are going to the police station from here to lodge a missing complaint for Neeraj. His cousin is coming to the police station as well, why don't you also come with us since you saw him last.'

Suddenly she looked distressed and teary-eyed. 'Sure, I have been so worried myself, I care so much about Neeraj, just as much as you guys do.' Emile, who had been watching the three of them with a distant politeness, stepped forward to comfort her. He and Maria spoke rapidly in Kannada before Emile switched to English. 'Do you want me to come along as well?' he asked in a perfunctory tone.

May 7, 11.15 pm

When the evening failed to yield Neeraj, Neelam Grover called his flatmate Haresh Sondarva. 'I had no idea she didn't know,' Haresh was to say later. 'I told her Neeraj had not been traceable since morning and that a missing complaint had been lodged. I should have been more careful instead of just blurting that out.'

By the next morning Amarnath Grover and his brother-in-law Satnam Arora were on a JetLite flight from Lucknow to Mumbai.

May 8, Mumbai

Amarnath Grover had not expected to be back in Mumbai so soon. Just two months ago he and Neelam had visited Ginni during Holi. He had entertained them wonderfully, taking them on the set of his mother's favourite serial, introducing them to his friends, and also to his then girlfriend. She was a fashion designer and had studied with Haresh. Ginni told them he wanted to marry her. 'After which both of you also come and live with me in Mumbai. You've worked long enough,' he'd said, accepting no argument.

So this was how power shifted centre. Their boy had become his own man. That night, talking in whispers as they lay next to each other, the Grovers planned for the future. They'd sell the Kanpur house—Shikha was already well settled and happy with her family—and move to Mumbai. 'Maybe we can look at a wedding date in December,' suggested Neelam.

On their return to Kanpur, at his wife's insistence, Amarnath Grover had spoken to a buyer for the bungalow. But now Ginni had gone missing, and he was headed to the police station to locate his child. Power may be deft, but responsibility was leaden-footed; it would always be his.

They went straight from the airport to the Malad police station where he met Neeraj's friends Nishant Lal and Deepak Kumar, and his flatmates Haresh and Sushant, all of whom he had been introduced to during his last trip. A missing complaint had been registered the previous day, the inspector-in-charge told him. He also heard that his son had last been to a flat belonging to one of his friends, a girl called Maria Susairaj. 'She lives close by,' said Haresh. 'She had called Neeraj at night to help her shift.'

'Let's go to her house then,' he said to Neeraj's flatmates. 'I'd like to meet and talk to her.'

Ginni had never mentioned this girl. When he asked Haresh about her, he mumbled something, clearly uncomfortable. Maria's flat was completely empty. 'That's strange,' Amarnath Grover thought to himself. 'Hadn't the girl called Ginni to help in the shifting? If so, where was her stuff?'

There was also evidence of some wet paint, which struck Haresh as odd. Normally tenants always ensured a house was painted before they took possession. But all those thoughts vanished as Maria started to weep. 'Why are you guys questioning me like this? I am also upset about Neeraj. If you want I'll come with you to the police station again.' Sushant tried to console her. 'It's okay, Maria, take it easy, we're all a little on the. . .' He stopped short when a stranger walked into the room and stood behind Maria, holding her shoulder comfortingly.

'Uh, this is Emile, my fiancé,' she said sniffling.

Neeraj's two flatmates gaped at one another, and after a hurried goodbye, shepherded Amarnath Grover out of the house.

May 9, morning

All of Neeraj's friends—Amarnath Grover hadn't realized just how popular his son was—eddied around him; their youthful energy, optimism, and determination inuring him against the anxiety that threatened to seep into his bones. 'Uncle, we'll keep up the pressure on the police, don't worry, we won't rest till they find Neeraj,' Deepak Kumar assured him as they got into the autorickshaw to go to Malad police station again for an update. At the police station Amarnath Grover spotted a familiar face. 'I see you on television every night, I like your style of reporting,' he told IBN7 reporter Nishat Shamsi, and then asked, 'Are the police telling you something that they're keeping from us?'

'They'll say something only if they make any progress. I think they're just playing the wait-and-watch game for now, and not doing much to locate Neeraj. Sir, why don't you go to Rakesh Maria instead?' Nishat Shamsi suggested helpfully.

May 9, 5.30 pm

In his imposing office at the Mumbai police headquarters at Crawford Market, the Joint Commissioner and head of the elite Crime Branch, had just been debriefed on an exasperating murder case that his boys from Unit IX had solved. The unidentified body of a young man had been found inside Joggers' Park at Lokhandwala in North Mumbai. The Crime Branch had traced it back to Chandigarh and found that the deceased, looking to emigrate to Canada, had paid a Mumbai-based travel agent for his services. When he found no progress on his travel papers he had come to Mumbai to demand the money back, only to be murdered by the fraudulent agent.

Rakesh Maria was talking to journalists about the killing and the surge in white-collar crime at his daily media briefing, dubbed 'The Durbar' by cheeky reporters, for his imperious style of communication, when his aide brought in a chit from a visitor.

In place of the name of the visitor it read: 'Father of Missing Boy.'

Intrigued, Maria summoned the visitor. 'There was something moving and dignified about Mr Grover, and as I heard the details of how his son had gone missing, an instinct told me this was not a simple case,' he was to later say in an interview.

Rakesh Maria, who saw the rise and decimation of the Mumbai underworld at close hand, is one of the most high-profile officers in the Mumbai police. He is a tall, burly man of middle age with a brisk, energetic manner and large eyes that miss little. His instinct, renowned in the criminal world, is extraordinary. One such hunch had led him to unravel the Mumbai blasts case in 1993, and is well documented in both Hussain S. Zaidi's book *Black Friday* and Suketu Mehta's *Maximum City*.

On March 12, 1993 a series of blasts had ripped through Mumbai. It was the biggest case in Mumbai's crime history and the police commissioner had asked Rakesh Maria to investigate it. He was then the deputy commissioner of police, Traffic. Two days after the commissioner called him in, his men had defused a bomb found in a scooter abandoned at Dadar railway station.

Maria held a late night meeting with twenty of the best police investigators in town and set them to work. Within five hours he had his first suspect. A Maruti van had been found abandoned with detonators near the Siemens office at Worli. The policemen who found the car had not paid heed to it, thinking the driver had abandoned the vehicle just before the checkpoint. Maria asked for the van to be checked, and to see its papers. The registration papers showed the van belonged to Mushtaq 'Tiger' Memon. When a team of investigators reached Memon's house in Mahim, they found the house was empty, and the cops found nothing except the key to a Bajaj scooter. As Rakesh Maria stared at that key, something clicked. He remembered the scooter bomb that had been defused at Dadar station two days ago. One of his men was asked to go and try the key on that scooter. It fit—nailing the little-known mastermind of the Mumbai blasts.

He had no answers to Neeraj Grover's mysterious disappearance yet, just a gut feeling. Rakesh Maria decided then and there that the Crime Branch would get involved in the investigation. 'I could see that Mr Grover was in distress and I did not want him to run around further, so instead of directing him to Unit XI which handles all

Crime Branch cases between Goregaon and Gorai further north, I sent an aide to call back the Unit IX team which had just left after briefing me about the murder at Lokhandwala.'

Mumbai police owes the legend of the force being second only to Scotland Yard, to an Englishman, Stephen Meredyth Edwardes, Mumbai's police commissioner in 1909. Edwardes, having studied the workings of Scotland Yard at first hand, set up the Criminal Investigation Department, which later became the Mumbai Crime Branch. The Crime Branch, divided into twelve units along the length of the city for administrative reasons, has the authority to do a parallel probe on any case registered in any Mumbai police station.

Freed from the often time-consuming administrative work of a police station, Crime Branch cops, usually to be found in plain clothes, work exclusively as detectives and have distinguished themselves by solving some of the most talked about cases in recent history, including the Gulshan Kumar murder and the J.J. Hospital shootout case. The notorious serial killer Charles Sobhraj was also arrested in a Crime Branch operation.

On May 13, four days after he ordered the probe, a group of Neeraj's friends came to see Rakesh Maria to complain about the lag in investigation. Among them was a young woman who sat right across him. There was something about her eyes that bothered him.

'What's your name?'

'Maria Susairaj, I am also a friend of Neeraj's.'

'I know, he disappeared from your house. You, lady,' Rakesh Maria leaned forward, stared hard and, pointing a finger straight at Maria Susairaj said, 'are my number one suspect.'

~

Amarnath Grover left Rakesh Maria's office and began the traumatic process of looking for Neeraj. He visited railway tracks, hospitals, mortuaries, and one evening even went to the Sanjay Gandhi National Park, foraging through parts of the forest spread over a hundred kilometres. Each trip began with dread and ended in momentary exultation: none of the bodies he was shown were his son's. The relief lasted but a few minutes.

He asked the local cable channel to run a ticker scroll offering a one lakh rupee reward to anyone with information on Neeraj, and personally went to each of the shanties on the road leading to Dheeraj Solitaire, stacked up against each other like uneven teeth, with Neeraj's picture to ask if anyone recalled having seen him. An urchin was lowered into the septic tanks of Maria's building to check for a body.

Amarnath Grover and Satnam Arora had a hundred posters printed with Neeraj's picture, with the word 'MISSING' in bold lettering. On a May afternoon of long shadows, Neeraj's father went to Dheeraj Solitaire and painstakingly put them up—on walls, on pillars, on the gates of neighbouring buildings, under car wipers, on shop shutters, on telephone poles, as if turning the area into a shrine for his missing son. Wherever the eye travelled there was Neeraj looking down, smiling gently.

That afternoon he saw Maria emerge from the building accompanied by her brother and sister; it was only the second time he had seen her. She looked around and then at him, standing there with the poster in one hand and a bottle of glue in the other, and got into an autorickshaw and rode past without saying anything.

There were also things about Ginni that he was just beginning to discover. As if by going missing, Ginni was offering an invitation to get to know him better. The girls. The smoking. The possibility of drugs. All the things that parents spend a lifetime living in denial of.

Maria had told the Malad police that Neeraj used ecstasy and crystal meth recreationally. At a friend's behest a police officer was sent to the Osho commune at Pune to find out if Neeraj had checked himself in.

Ginni's credit card details were scanned—they revealed nothing. They examined his bank account. The last withdrawal was for Rs 1,000 on May 5, two days before Ginni's disappearance, and the last deposit had been the Rs 10,000 that he himself had sent his son. Amarnath Grover called up his wife in Kanpur, unable to keep the despair out of his voice. 'Ginni bas gayab ho gaya hai' (Our son has just disappeared). He took to waking up and heading straight to the Unit IX office on Hill Road in Bandra day after day, his anxious presence reminding the police that his son was still missing.

But all this while, without Amarnath Grover's knowledge, Inspector Satish Raorane, the investigating officer in the case, and his team were working on their suspect. On May 17, her twenty-eighth birthday, Maria was called to the police station in Bandra and questioned for over ten hours.

Two days later, Amarnath Grover walked into the Unit IX office as usual. As he sat sipping chai and waiting for the officers in the corridor outside, he saw Satish Raorane emerge from one of the rooms. Before he could go up to him with his daily plea, Raorane walked up to him, smiling. 'Mr Grover, please relax. I request you, don't come here for the next few days. I will personally inform you of the developments.'

Buoyed, he immediately called Neelam. 'The inspector told me to relax. I think they are getting some news of Ginni, why don't you also come to Mumbai?' He ignored Raorane's advice but found the office of unit IX mostly deserted over the next two days. 'Where's everybody?' he asked the chaiwallah he had befriended. 'Aap hi ke kaam se gaye hain' (They are out for your work), he was informed.

It was the evening of May 21. Amarnath and Neelam Grover had just left the Unit IX office, looking at another restless night stretch ahead when Amarnath's phone rang. It was Rakesh Maria. 'Mr Grover, where are you?'

'Just outside the Unit IX office in Bandra, sir.'

'Why don't you please go back, sit there for a while.'

Rakesh Maria had just finished briefing the media about the Neeraj Grover case. It was imperative to speak to Amarnath Grover before he switched on the television. None of his boys had the heart to speak to the old man, and the task fell to the boss. 'Mr Grover, please go back to the Unit IX office. I am sorry but your son is dead. We have found out what happened.'

In the blur that followed there were moments of piercing clarity. Neeraj's friends rushing over to get them home, the clutch of Neelam's hand threatening to crack his knuckles, and the avid faces of television reporters, on channel after channel.

This, above all.

Sometime after Neelam Grover's nightly conversation with Neeraj, and before her morning call to him, their son had been stabbed to death in Maria Susairaj's flat, his body violated. The police claimed that Maria along with her fiancé, the naval officer Emile Jerome, had killed Ginni—after which they had dragged his body into the bathroom and hacked it up. 'Into bits,' said Rakesh Maria. Television reporters, citing their own sources, claimed it was into three hundred pieces.

Returning dazed to the flat their son had inhabited until a few days ago, Amarnath Grover and Neelam watched the reporters hyperventilate on screen. 'Aur uske baad, they hacked the body into three hundred pieces, stuffed it into three large carry bags, and dumped them in the jungles off Manor and set them on fire.' This end for their beautiful son?

'Will we get something to do a cremation with?' Amarnath Grover asked the policeman accompanying them to the Nagpada Police Hospital the next day, where he and Neelam had to give DNA samples, before going on to answer his own question, 'After three hundred pieces what would be left?'

Later, back at the Malad police station, where Maria Susairaj and Emile Jerome had been brought before being taken to jail, the media was like a panting beast. Neelam Grover had spent the night surfing for news of Ginni's death, astonished to see it being discussed so authoritatively. Motive? History? Consequence? Equations? They knew nothing. She knew nothing.

Through a small barred window in the room where she waited at the Malad police station, she saw Maria and Emile being brought in. Their faces were covered with black hoods. In the darkened room, the only illusion of light was their pale-coloured clothing, and they looked disembodied, but only until a policeman came in and switched on the tube light. For a moment, just a moment, Maria Susairaj lifted her hood and blinked.

2

Maria

'I live for today; tomorrow if I don't wake up forgive me for my sins.'

—Maria Susairaj

Jhooth, Maria's 2002 debut film, opens with the camera lingering on her swaying posterior as she walks to college with an exaggeratedly sexy gait, dressed in a form-fitting micro-mini, big platform shoes, and cheap flesh-coloured tights—a legacy of the egregious eighties. When the camera finally pans on her face, it reveals a plain broad visage, an oddly flattened nose, and a mouth full of teeth. Yet, undeniably, she exudes a certain ripeness playing a spoilt young girl who toys with the boys. Crudely, the film approximates her image both in Mysore when she was in college, and later in Bangalore during her brief stint in the Kannada film industry.

Her looks have changed considerably since that time: her teeth have been fixed, drastic weight loss has reduced her from voluptuous to petite, the hair is longer, and her nose appears noticeably sharper. But through the changes she has retained the ineffable sensuality that leaves men either uneasy or completely disarmed in her presence.

'She was sentimental, flirtatious—most of her friends were male—and she often wore sexy dresses. In short, I can say, she was a complete woman,' recalled Hemanth Kashyap, an old classmate from Mysore with touching naïveté. While describing her lifestyle in Mysore, she told a former lover: 'When everybody was walking, I was on a cycle, when people were on cycles, I was on a bike, and when people were on bikes, I was riding in a car.'

'Actually she drove a Kinetic to Mahajana College,' retorted former classmate Abhinanth Kumar. 'She was very conscious about wearing branded clothing and while she was no doubt sweet and helpful, one always got the feeling that she only wanted to mingle with the elite, like the wealthy sons of coffee planters from Coorg.' Rumours of her liaisons with the Coorg gang boys, who were called Ka12 because of their licence plates, enlivened Mysore for many. Yet, push for details and the stories don't hold up.

When Emile asked his parents for permission to marry Maria, they declined strenuously.

Prominent Mysore dentist Dr Anil Thomas, who was once a close friend of Maria's uncle Santunesan, offered an explanation quoting the parish grapevine: 'She was older than him, an actress, and then there was the whole issue of the family—Emile's parents are old Malayalee Christians from Wayanad. They may be wealthy, but Monica's family's Christian roots barely go back two generations; they are converts,' he told me as he downed a chhota peg at the Mysore Golf Club. At that his friend, who is from the same parish as Maria's family, interjected, 'Also, have you seen her? So dark! She used to wear weird clothes; she was no match for Emile.'

In a small town, a whisper travels further than a shout. In Mysore, rumours about Maria will not be shushed, and bear with them all the prejudices of gender, colour, and class.

But the disparagement extends to both sides. 'I never encouraged Mysoreans,' Maria once told me, alluding to the men. 'Their whole attitude is: "Uper se tapki hai, kha lo isse" [Women are to be plucked, like low-hanging fruit]. Any woman who goes out to work there is fair game.'

For nearly three years I had been trying to persuade Maria to do an interview for this book. While always pleasant, she never fully acquiesced until a few days before the sessions court judgment in which she would be convicted. The tension in the courtroom had been thickening over the days as Emile's and her lawyers spun their competing narratives, pitching the lovers as adversaries.

The morning that she finally agreed to speak to me, Emile's advocate Wahab Khan had made his final arguments with considerable flourish. In the sparsely attended courtroom, Wahab, a man of formidable physical heft, pulled the small tabletop lectern towards him and rested his weight on the fragile prop. Next, he pulled one foot out of his scruffy, unpolished shoes, the backs of which were bent out of shape from frequent abuse, and balanced it on the wooden chair in front of him.

Poised like a combative wrestler, he raised his voice and launched into the most compelling argument he would present as Emile Jerome's attorney. There was nothing to prove that Neeraj Grover wasn't already dead when Emile walked into his girlfriend's Mumbai flat on the morning of May 7, 2008.

'Who lived in the flat? Maria!'

'Who knew Neeraj Grover? Maria!'

'Who had Neeraj last been seen with? Maria!'

His rising decibel level startled the pigeons cooing on the lintels outside the windows, and shattered the post-lunch torpor of the courtroom. Special Judge and Additional Sessions Judge M.W. Chandwani widened his eyes imperceptibly. The onus was now on the prosecution, Wahab thundered, to prove that Neeraj had been alive at 7.30 am when his client entered the building.

'They have not been able to prove any motive so far as Emile is concerned, and if there was any motive to commit murder, it was Maria who may have had one.'

At the end of proceedings that day, Maria agreed to talk. I wondered if Emile's turnaround had made her change her mind. 'Even a monkey, when cornered, drops her baby,' she said with equanimity. 'We're human beings. A man and a woman.'

She spoke as if delivering catechism—'I live for today; tomorrow if I don't wake up forgive me for my sins'; 'Never act in life in such a manner that you leave no room for second chances.' Later, going through my notes, I realized she hadn't been speaking so much as reviewing her life.

Vanity and affability have long been twin features of Maria's persona. An old boyfriend, Pavan Kumar, described her as kind and caring, and excellent with children. Like some of Maria's other boyfriends he is also tall, with a dancer's athleticism. It was through Pavan that she met the choreographer Deepak Singh, in whose flat she stayed in Mumbai, and Kiran Shreyans, whose car she borrowed. 'She could be a doll. While we were in a relationship, she would often sing for me—in those moments I felt something like love for her,' said Pavan. The two met in 2004, two years after *Jhooth* was released, when she came to Studio 5678—the dance training centre he ran in Bangalore—wanting to learn salsa. She was working on a music video for a private album of her songs and was in a hurry to learn the dance, insisting on private tuitions.

Her debut film had failed, but the currency of its songs gave her enough recognition for Pavan to offer to train her himself. 'She was a good-looking girl—graceful—she dressed up really well and she stood out in class. What people could learn in three–four months, she learnt within a month. Before long, we were in a relationship.'

They were together for a year during which time Pavan came to believe that she had rebounded into their relationship after breaking up with another choreographer from the Kannada film industry who had abused her. Though physically intimate, Pavan found it difficult to connect with Maria emotionally. 'She was a bright girl who only liked to talk about herself. She liked herself very much and spent a lot of time in front of the mirror.'

There's the hint of iron filings in his hair and stubble, and he speaks with a candour borne of confidence, but the thirty-six-year-old recalled a younger, more uncertain self when Maria's mercurial temperament had him at odds. 'She would be quite romantic with me in the evening but if I brought it up the next morning, she would grow cold, saying, "I don't want to hear anything about that".' He was hurt by her refusal to publicly acknowledge him as her boyfriend. He was introduced to her family—she took him home to Mysore for Christmas, and would also take him along to auditions and business meetings, 'But if anyone asked whether we were seeing each other, she always said, "No".'

'Monica never liked being part of a group. I, on the other hand, liked to hang out with my friends. She'd join us but contribute little to the conversation.' Even when she was alone with Pavan, Maria liked her space. 'Though we were going steady, she didn't want us to be together at all times. "I just wanted you in my bed," she told him once. But [she] then immediately held my hand, and said she'd been joking.' What Pavan found most difficult to accept was her secrecy. 'Often she'd go out but refuse to tell me where she was going or who she was meeting.' She was playing an unfair game, he felt, where only she knew the rules.

In the absence of a strong emotional connection, sex became a tool to navigate the relationship, and with it came the attendant urge to inflict cruelty on one another. 'There was a girl in the class I ran at Indira Nagar who was attracted to me, and I casually went out with her a couple of times. This made Monica jealous and she immediately got back at me by flirting outrageously with my friends.' Remarkably open about her past relationships, she would tease him with details he had no wish to hear. 'She had no regrets about any of them, saying it just happened. I'd often tell her, "Leave it, Monica, I don't want to hear any of this," but she would just laugh.'

Exhausted by these skirmishes, the couple began to drift apart. When a year later, in 2005, Maria announced that she wanted to move to Mumbai to pursue a career in Bollywood, Pavan did not ask her to stay. By this time two of her other films, *Excuse Me* and *OK, Sir, OK*, released in 2003 and 2004, had also failed, and she had begun doing item numbers. 'I thought she had a better chance of succeeding in Bangalore than in Mumbai, where the girls are better and the competition far tougher, but I chose not to say this to her.'

Instead, playing the solicitous boyfriend, Pavan called up his old friends from Studio 5678, Deepak and Kiran, who had since shifted to Mumbai, and asked them to help her find her feet in the city.

These days Maria's maternal grandfather Philomen Raj is rarely seen around Bannimantap, the posh enclave in Mysore that he helped build. Neighbours say old age and ill health keep him inside his sprawling corner bungalow, but his presence can still be felt in town. Aside from the buildings he has constructed, most of his nine children still live in the vicinity—his corporator son Santunesan's house with his red-beacon cars is right next door, and Maria's parents live across the road.

Philomen Raj had migrated from Pondicherry to Mysore in the 1950s to tap into the first boom of nation-building, and set up his own construction firm soon after he arrived. Some years later he was joined by his wife's impoverished cousin Joseph Susairaj, Maria's father, who came from Bangalore to improve his circumstances and support his five siblings. Though Joseph started as a mere writer—industry jargon for accountant—their partnership prospered, and so did the company. Raj Constructions soon became one of the leading building firms in southern Karnataka and it seemed logical to Philomen Raj to deepen his relationship with Joseph. Unlike in north India, where it would be considered incestuous, the alliance between maternal uncle and niece is seen as most auspicious in Tamil culture. The niece is 'mora ponnu', literally translated as 'my girl'.

So Joseph married his cousin's daughter Nirmala in 1976, but just two years later he fell out with Philomen Raj and broke rank with his father-in-law to set up his own company. There is no evidence of subsequent acrimony, but when Hindu–Muslim riots broke out in Mysore in 1986, Joseph Susairaj had wanted his immediate family to leave Bannimantap, and stayed on only at his wife's insistence.

'While we were growing up, Father constantly shuttled between Mysore and Bangalore, working terribly hard to establish the business,' Maria's older brother Richard told me. At thirty-one, he was the eldest of Joseph Susairaj's three children, followed two years apart by Maria Monica and Maria Veronica, or Moni and Roni as the sisters were called. Richard, who is petite like his sisters, sketches a picture of an idyllic childhood spent with a large extended family. 'Several of my aunts are nearly of our age so we were a large group, often going to Ooty for family picnics, and to the church every Sunday.'

Although Joseph Susairaj was often out of town on business, he compensated for his absence by indulging his children. 'Everything we wanted, we got.' Except there would be no wriggling out of catechism class. Already religious, Joseph's belief grew as his new company earned a slew of contracts from churches and other Christian institutions. Though himself a Roman Catholic, his clients cut across denominations. 'We've built for Jesuits, Protestants, Anglicans, CSI Dioceses, as also secular institutions like the National Aerospace Laboratories,' Richard said. His wife and his mother Nirmala also run a primary school in Mysore, St Peter's Educational Institution. The emphasis on religiosity was extraordinary, he explained, smiling wryly, his cognac-coloured eyes—remarkably like Maria's—softening at the memory. 'Our parents were very strict about Sunday Mass, special religious classes, and everyday evening prayers. In each and every walk of life we were made to know our limits.'

While Richard pursued a diploma in civil engineering before joining his father's firm, and Veronica a master's in computer science, Maria Monica was the artist of the family, and in turn was entitled to the licence that comes with being one. Time with her father may have been at a premium but Maria grew up to be a daddy's girl. 'She talked a lot about him coming up in life the hard way, often saying, "I really love my father, if it weren't for him we would not have this life",' Geeta Narayana, a neighbour who grew up next door to Maria told me. When Geeta's father, Mysore's acclaimed inlay-work artist P. Gorraiya, visited the family after Maria's arrest, he found Joseph distraught. 'Susairaj just kept weeping and saying he wished he were dead. He always completely supported Monica in whatever she had wanted to do; he wished for all his children to become self-sufficient.'

'When we were growing up Monica would be always busy. Arangetram, singing, correspondence courses, modelling for jewellery showrooms, belly dancing, it was always something or the other,' Geeta recalled. That, and Geeta's own preoccupations prevented them from being close. This strain comes up in all interviews about Maria—she was friendly but had few friends, and most attribute this to her secretive nature. 'Even my parents would knock on my door before entering my room, but that's the respect they afforded us children,' she said once. Her closest confidante remained her sister Veronica. 'In the time I was with her I didn't meet a single of Monica's friends,' Pavan recalled. 'Which was a bit strange because most people have a best friend, but she told me she liked to be alone.'

Only Richard hints at a contrary impulse. 'Moni was an outspoken girl, very free with her expression.' It is something he said several times during our conversation, at one point almost with wonder—perhaps grappling to better understand his own sister and later events, especially in the two weeks between Neeraj's disappearance and her arrest, when the police hounded them every day. And yet despite all his protests, Maria had been secretive with Richard too. Her brother admitted that throughout the ordeal she had kept the family in the dark about Neeraj's death.

Richard and Veronica had taken the first flight out to Mumbai after Maria called home complaining of police harassment. When they landed, Richard asked Maria what Emile had been doing there, and she told him he had come 'to see the new house and to spend a couple of days with me'. Richard, who spent most of his time with his father in Bangalore, claimed he had never even seen Emile until the trial began. After Maria's arrest, he put his life and career on hold, flying to Mumbai every few weeks to visit Maria in jail, or to see her in the court. 'She's our girl, it's not easy being inside the jail.'

On the day of her release from prison when a frenzied media chased her all over Mumbai, it was Richard who stood by her side. Yet, for all their apparent closeness, there are gaps in the family narrative. When they left for Mumbai on May 8, 2008, Richard and Veronica told their father that they were going to Mumbai because Maria was unwell. He was kept in the dark even when his wife joined her children in Mumbai a few days later. 'I just thought that since Moni drives fast quite often she may have had an accident or something,' Joseph said, claiming he didn't know that Maria did not have a car in Mumbai. 'I came to know of what happened when I read the newspaper on May 22 like everybody else.'

He seems more baffled than angry by the truancy of his daughter. 'It seems you cannot say anything to children these days. Her lifestyle changed after she came to Mumbai.

We were not keen on Monica joining films. The film line is very different; they have no fixed timings, they shoot at odd hours. I was doing business and was very busy, so some servant would go with her to the set, but she would often get lonely after she'd come back from work. The problem is when your children have some talent, you can't not allow their talent to grow. She wanted to be famous from very early on. From our end we did everything we could, we kept her busy with many classes, we gave her a vehicle, we gave her a driver.'

'We thought she'd do one or two films and then settle down. When she told me she liked Emile and wanted to marry him, I said okay, and sent one of my friends to talk to his parents—but they refused. "What can we do," I told her, "they've refused, forget him." But she wanted to shift to Mumbai again; they both had plans to settle there.' Mysteriously Joseph Susairaj too says that he himself never met Emile. When I asked him if he had ever spoken to Maria about Neeraj's death, he said: 'I thought I would hurt her feelings if I spoke to her about the incident, so I never did.'

Even Richard is cautious. 'She needed to know Neeraj better before taking his help and expecting him to get her roles. She understands what we are going through and what we expect of her.' When I asked him what that is, he said somewhat abruptly, 'We expect her to know what has happened is wrong.' When I persisted, he clammed up. 'Please,' he pleaded, 'all these emotions are new, there is nothing else I have to say.'

Maria was not yet five when she started lessons in Bharatanatyam, and she took to dance naturally. She gave several performances and was written about in the local newspapers as 'Baby Monica'. By the time she was an adolescent at her middle school in St Mathias (which was built by her father), Maria was the school star. In addition to her prosperous family background, she was a talented singer, reasonably good at her studies, and a Bharatanatyam dancer of exceptional grace. She carried herself with the toffee-nosed confidence that such knowledge gives adolescent girls.

But even in those days, Maria didn't want to focus on one thing alone. 'Full-fledged dance can also consume your life,' she said. 'I have many interests and I wanted to be a freelancer for myself.' So she also trained as a Carnatic vocalist while still at school before going to Europe and China on a cultural exchange programme. She was studying for a BA in journalism, but cut it short for her film career that began when she was still in her second year of university. 'She didn't attend any classes that year,' recalled her classmate Hemanth Kashyap. In all she worked in four Kannada films, *Jhooth, Excuse Me, OK, Sir, OK,* and *Ekdant,* in which she played a journalist. Her acting was stilted, reflecting none of the fluidity that marked her dance.

'None of her films were big hits,' Richard said. But while she often spoke of joining her father's business as an interior decorator, and struggled to find roles, Maria never thought of giving up her showbiz dream. Her brother agreed: 'Were I to compare myself with Moni, I'd say if I didn't do well at something, I'd try and do something else. But she was very ambitious in what she wanted to do. It's not a bad quality,' he said, his face opaque, 'to perfect yourself.'

Richard himself had been against Maria's acting career, and when she still went ahead he stopped speaking to her. 'In that entire year when *Jhooth* was being made, he did not speak to me. But once the film released, he went to a cinema hall all by himself and came back and hugged me, saying, "Well tried",' Maria told me as we stood talking outside the court a few days before the verdict.

Through all of this their mother Nirmala remained a shadowy presence in the background. The one time she did break her reticence to protest was in 2005, when Maria announced that she was moving to Mumbai for what would be her first stint there. Nirmala Susairaj had watched Maria become her own woman, stubbornly pursuing her ambitions, but while the Kannada film industry was in their backyard—Maria's father could keep an eye on her in Bangalore—Mumbai was a foreign country. 'She asked me if there was any way I could stop Monica from going there,' said Saurav, a Mysore boy who starred opposite her in *Jhooth*. He called Maria's mother the gentlest of women. 'Her mother would say, "Tell Moni there is nothing wrong with working in Kannada films. You too are working here, aren't you?" She was most unwilling to let her go to Mumbai.'

But Maria prevailed, as she so often did. What's more, she got her mother to accompany her to Mumbai where the acting coach Asha Chandra would not accept students unless they arrived with a guardian. 'I told her, "You're already an actress, why do you need classes, and if you want to improve yourself, use Kannada films as training, and learn,'" said Saurav, who himself went on to do small parts in Hindi films with Zayed Khan and Emraan Hashmi. When he bumped into Maria at Juhu beach a couple of years later, he said he was shocked by her drastic physical transformation from the time they had debuted together. 'But at that time I could see she was quite set on going to Mumbai.'

Movie buffs of a certain vintage are familiar with the acting coach Asha Chandra, who regularly graced the pages of film glossies in the company of her protégés Dimple Kapadia, Sunny Deol, and Jackie Shroff in the 1980s. She stood out for her bumblebee frames and crescent-like eyebrows, which hung over mildly surprised bug eyes. But an encounter with Osho, and the demise of the 'formula' in Bollywood—brothers separated at a mela, or the hero and the heroine dancing around trees—saw her fade from the public eye. However, her past successes ensure a steady trickle of aspirants from towns like Mysore, Tonk, and Ratlam to her Juhu office—a cavernous room behind a black soundproofed door with black curtains, black sofas, a black marble floor, and marble walls on which hang pithy sayings framed in, well, black—'To Be Trusted Is A Greater Compliment Than To Be Loved.' 'If You Tell The Truth You Don't Have To Remember Anything.'

It was in this bizarre all-black apartment which had been converted into an actors' studio that Maria and Nirmala

Susairaj found themselves, and Nirmala watched her daughter excitedly complete the admission formalities, fluttering away from her like a breakaway kite.

I went to see Asha Chandra four years later to talk about Maria. She sailed into the same room in which she had met Maria and her mother. Dressed in a flowing lavender caftan, she was perched primly on a moulded plastic chair behind a schoolteacher's desk—only the ruler was missing.

'Madam, how can I help you?'

'Do you remember Maria Susairaj,' I asked.

'You bet.'

'She came to me four years ago with her mother. I insist that applicants be accompanied by guardians, because I do not want any runaways.' She rummaged through the drawers and fished out a folder with Maria's application form along with a picture of her and Nirmala Susairaj, who looks clearly discomfited. 'Maria was very ambitious but not terribly talented. But I don't look for anything before accepting students, madam, because these days anyone can become a star.'

However, in her prospectus she issues a somewhat dire warning to those with misguided aspirations: 'No rosy picture is drawn of the film industry for students and they are told that if they work hard and have respect for the film industry, the industry has place for each one—hence if they are here just to while away time and money, they may as well go home.'

She went on to give me a grand tour of the Asha Chandra Acting Institute, which was spread over two floors of the middle class apartment block. On the higher floor were the living quarters for outstation students. 'Separate for girls and boys,' she rapped out sharply. On the lower level two flats had been merged to create the workshop floor. We walked past a tiny kitchen heavily stacked with steel utensils into a large hall that was as brightly lit as the office was dark. A mirror hung across the length of a wall further accentuated its brightness. On the remaining walls hung life-sized posters of her star students—an unknown hunk lounging James Dean style in tight jeans and vest, caught my eye.

She looked at the poster and sighed dramatically, 'That's Manish. You must know about him and Maria.' I feigned deep insight and hazarded a non-committal line, 'Um... Hmm. Quite sad, no...'

'Terrible. That boy was heartbroken.' Manish (this is an assumed name to protect his identity) was in the same batch as Maria. He came from a well-to-do family in Tonk, Rajasthan, and bore a striking resemblance to John Abraham. After winning a male beauty contest, he was selected by the director Saawan Kumar Tak for a film. Tak sent him to Asha Chandra's class for the three-month course.

'He was promising, that boy, and then he got involved with Maria. She manipulated boys. Was always friendly with the men in the group but hardly interacted with the girls. Manish told me they later moved in together, but before that, while she was still in the hostel here, there was a small scandal when she went off to Goa for a holiday with another boy, the son of an influential police officer. She had told me she had to go home to Bangalore. I always found her clever but not intelligent.'

'Was any action taken against the transgression?' I asked.

'Darling!'—within twenty minutes I had gone from a starchy 'madam' to a filmi endearment—'I restrict my interest to the professional, to what's happening in class. That hole down there, I am not its keeper.' Maria needed to correct her yin and yang, the new-age spiritualist and Osho acolyte said. The last Asha Chandra heard from Maria was some months after she finished the course. 'She called me one day and said she had some auditions this side of town, and could she come and stay at the hostel for one night. "I'll pay the rent for one night," she said, but disappeared the next morning without doing so. After that I only read about her in the newspapers.' When I asked Maria about Asha Chandra, she said tartly, 'She was dumped by a man and has turned bitter and crazy since.'

For choreographer Deepak Singh and Kiran Shreyans, who had helped her find a flat at Vanrai Colony in Goregaon East at Pavan's request, Manish's presence in Maria's life created a rather awkward situation. 'We knew her as our friend Pavan's girlfriend but here she was living in with someone else,' recalled Kiran.

She had also begun calling Pavan in Bangalore to tell him all about Manish. 'She'd try and make me jealous, but I was already past caring,' he said. Kiran, his then long-time girlfriend, Manish and Maria became a foursome, socializing frequently, going out for films and occasional dinners. 'She was cool, poised, never seemed hassled about things like lack of money that is always an issue with most strugglers, but despite that there was something about her that I did not care for,' says Kiran. 'She was,' he paused, scouting for accurate words, 'secretive and complicated. No. The word I am looking for is shrewd. And I have to add, she always got good-looking boys.'

We were sitting in the veranda of the Renaissance Federation Club at Andheri where Kiran taught dance to a batch of mostly lissome, pretty women. I asked if he himself was ever attracted to her. His friend 'FS' who had been listening in intently let out a thunderclap of laughter. Kiran offered a quieter chuckle and then a fervent, 'No man!'

'But I can tell you why she's so attractive to the men. In the time we were studying in Mysore, girls would walk to college, head low, holding their books protectively across their chests. If they happened to look up from under downcast eyes, we were delighted, and if they also smiled, we'd be ecstatic, ladki pati. Monica's charms are somewhat like that—she's feminine, coy, seems a bit helpless, always conveying vulnerability. Urban women these days are so aggressive, independent—they want to compete with you, conquer you. In the face of such ferocity Monica's quietly feminine charms work, I guess.'

Maria and Kiran's friendship soured when she caused trouble between him and his then girlfriend, he said. He would not go into detail about the break-up, but the scars remained. 'Look at all the love stories, including the Neeraj–Monica–Emile triangle, have you ever heard any story where the woman goes crazy? It's always the men who go crazy in love; they have problems handling their emotions. And now with women getting so forward it has become impossible to find peace in relationships. There are no longer any rules for them. What's formal clothing is not defined for women. They can go out at all hours, they've become like men. What's more, society has begun to accept it. Take my own case. I didn't care that Monica—who was my friend's girlfriend—was seeing and living in with another man. Back home in Mysore she would have been socially ostracized, isolated, and would have thought ten times before doing something like this. All around me I see people getting together but rarely do I find them happy in those relationships. I wouldn't be surprised if a lot of the men turn gay because of the way women have become.'

Away from the screaming traffic of Worli, in a quiet, minimalist flat with a stunning, sweeping view of the Arabian Sea, Udayan Patel sat behind closed doors applying salve to many a bruised psyche. I was in the office of the famous psychotherapist—the best keeper of South Mumbai's secrets—to understand the complex triggers that lead us to crime, the psychology that lets someone cut up a body while maintaining a façade of normalcy.

Udayan chose a circumlocutory route to address the issue of what is normal, and what is not. He told me a story—a real one. During the 1992–3 riots, disturbed by what was going on in Mumbai during the time, he left the sanctuary of his home one day to step out for a walk and spotted three men standing aimlessly on the 'S' Bridge at Byculla. 'Something about their insouciance in the midst of such tension alerted me. I went up to them and started chatting. After a while, when they had confirmed that I was not a journalist, they asked if I wanted a colour television and a video cassette recorder for Rs 3,000. I asked them if it was loot ka maal, they said, "No, it's Musalman ka maal." I gathered the men were rioters and since I was interested in their psychology, I gave them my card and told them I was a 'bheje ka doctor,' and that if they ever wanted to, they could come and see me at no charge. They seemed sceptical. "We wouldn't need to," they said.

"You will," I countered. "When you can't sleep, when you will get headaches and when your upset stomach will not get better despite the medicines, you'll want to see me."'

A month after this meeting he got a call from one of the men, describing the exact symptoms. 'We spoke for a while until I asked him directly if he had participated in a killing. He admitted he had beaten up a man, slashed him with a sword, and then set him on fire. This man had then gone back home where his mother and sister had washed his bloodstained clothes and served him hot food. He ate well that day but soon after found his appetite deserting him.'

'I dream,' he told Udayan, 'that the dead man enters my body through the crevice between the nail and the skin of my toe and goes on to occupy my stomach. I have no appetite because he sits in my stomach, filling it.' The man had stopped eating and lost weight dramatically.

One of the side stories from Maria and Emile's murder trial at the Mumbai sessions court had been Maria's studiedly fashionable appearances. *Au courant* skinny pants, delicately patterned tops cinched at the waist emphasizing its smallness, high-heeled shoes, and impeccable make-up; it was as if denied a stab at stardom, Maria was determined to play a stellar role as herself for the news cameras. It even prompted her lawyer Sudeep Pasbola to once comment after an adjournment due to her late arrival in court, 'Madam, please get up earlier tomorrow to finish your make-up, and be in court on time.' (Pasbola later withdrew from the case after his junior was accused of trying to bribe an important prosecution witness to change her testimony in favour of Maria.)

But as the trial drew to a close, Maria began undergoing a transformation. She ballooned to twice her size, and started wearing drab clothes. She stopped using make-up and opted for flats over the high heels she usually wore. On several occasions it happened that people who peeped into the courtroom, prompted by sheer curiosity to see the actress, walked away tsking in disappointment.

One day, during a break in court proceedings while we stood talking, I offered to leave her alone so she could have lunch, but she told me not to bother. 'I just can't seem to eat these days, I have no appetite for food, though I can't stop binging on chocolates,' she said, pulling out a paper bag full of chocolate bars that was to be lunch and dinner. 'That's why I've become so big.'

This self-destructive behaviour was not new. Though she often covered them with bangles, she had unmistakable welts on her wrist that web across the length of her forearm. Since there is never any delicate way to ask such a question, I simply asked her whether she had ever tried to harm herself. 'There had been unrelenting pressure from my family to get married though I myself had no desire for marriage. On their prodding I saw some boys but it didn't work out. Then a few years ago, my sister-in-law organized for me to meet someone.' She took Manish along to the meeting. 'He sat at a table some distance away from us. So I met this bald man, at least ten years older than me, he was divorced but still in touch with his wife, and with whom he ran an advertising agency. I left within fifteen minutes of meeting him.'

Maria felt humiliated. For a girl who'd had especially good-looking boyfriends, the idea that her family believed this was the best she could get, was unpalatable. That night she slit her wrist. 'Don't worry,' she smiled, as we moved towards the police van that had come to collect her, 'I won't do it again, I love life too much.'

Choreographer Deepak Singh hinted that he saw the welts and cuts when he began to hang out with her in 2005. Less embittered than Kiran, he offered a more nuanced view of her. 'I always found her friendly, though somewhat abrupt. Like she did not even call up to say goodbye when she left for Bangalore after her first stint in Mumbai in 2005–6, despite the fact that we had helped her find a place here. At the same time she had no qualms asking for assistance once again when she was doing *Kuniyona Baara,* the Kannada version of the television show *Nach Baliye,* in 2007. First, she wanted to know who she should select as her partner, then later sought tips to fine-tune some dance moves. When I went to Bangalore briefly, I even went across to where she and her dance partner Vasanth were rehearsing and gave them a class.' But her time in television didn't last long. Maria rowed with the judges of the show, challenging their judgement during an episode, and walked out halfway through.

'She struck me as terribly confused about what she wanted to do in life. She always spoke about working with her father as an interior designer, but none of the qualifications she acquired were towards that. Instead she took classes in singing, belly dancing, Latin American dance, acting.' Nor did she show any urgency about trying to get work as an actress when she was first in Mumbai, Kiran told me. 'She didn't seem like a go-getter in terms of trying to get work.'

Maria didn't rush around studios or the offices of producers and directors, clawing for every bit of work like most strugglers. Her privileged life left her ill equipped for the rigours and humiliations of Bollywood. She found the notion of struggle romantic, but stopped at that. 'I saw fame back home as a young woman, and I always wanted to be a dancer, open my own dance academy. I am not some desperate-for-work starlet the media makes me out to be,' she told me. Instead, during the year of her first stint in Mumbai, Maria did what she knew best, she took classes from the eminent playback singer Suresh Wadkar. She also did a few print campaigns, including one for the Mumbai police, a public awareness campaign following the 2006 serial blasts on Mumbai's local trains.

It was within a few months of this that Maria first met Neeraj Grover. Contrary to police accounts that suggest she met Neeraj just a week before his death, Maria had met him during her first stay in Mumbai, at one of the hundreds of auditions she gave, and had found him attractive. But before their acquaintance could mature into something deeper, she was signed on by actor-director Sachin Pilgaonkar to play the second lead in his Kannada remake of the Marathi film *Ekdant*, and she returned to Bangalore to work on this film, not even informing Deepak Singh.

But Mumbai's allure remained deep-rooted and Maria returned in September 2007, and rented a flat in Dheeraj Solitaire, on the same floor as she would again in 2008 when Neeraj was killed. But within two months of this second Mumbai stint, she had packed her bags and moved back to Mysore, unable to resist her many contradictory impulses. By this time she had also started her long-distance relationship with Emile.

The handsome naval officer had been a friend of her sister's at school, and it was Veronica who found him on Orkut and decided that he would be a perfect match for Maria. After her suicide attempt the Susairaj family had backed off from trying to arrange a match and asked Maria to find herself a husband instead. She enrolled on shaadi.com, but eventually found Emile on the social networking site through Roni. 'I just saw his photograph and liked what I saw,' said Maria.

At the end of 2007, when Maria flew from Mumbai to London to visit her sister Veronica, Emile came to see her off and even took her to Lonavla where he had studied. After that they returned to Mumbai and spent a night together at the house of Maria's former neighbour at Dheeraj Solitaire, Mayuri Prajapati.

A few months on, in March 2008, Maria came back to Mumbai for another short visit. It was on this trip that she told Deepak Singh she was engaged, and went shopping with him for shirts for Emile. But on this trip she had also met up with Neeraj Grover again. He casually let her know of his proximity to the television doyenne Ekta Kapoor, and with that merest hint of promise, all the old pulls came alive. At twenty-eight, this would be Maria's last chance at stardom: a time to redeem the possibilities that had once seemed her prerogative.

3

Emile

'If there is one word to capture Emile's personality, I'd use the word stud.'

—One of Emile's course mates in the navy

NOTHING ACCENTUATES THE difference between small town and big city more than the fading twilight. It is the hour when the city starts to shimmer for the night ahead. At dusk, small towns start winding down—the familiar shops shut, and twilight hangs heavy as the sound of television soaps resounds oppressively, echoing a collective boredom.

On one such evening, Vinay Kumar S., who now works at a medical transcription business in Mysore, met Emile Jerome. They had studied together in the same school as Maria Susairaj. 'Emile was my best friend through school, and we have remained friends since. Every time he came to Mysore on leave, he'd spend a couple of days with me.' The last time they saw each other, three months before Neeraj's death, Vinay took a photograph of Emile on his cellphone. The naval officer looked handsome in his purple shirt, his posture erect. But it is his expression that arrested attention—at once slightly quizzical and ironically amused, as if he were biting back a chuckle.

'We were in a coffee shop talking, as men often do, about girls, specifically the ones we knew. I don't know what prompted me, but I said to him, "Can you imagine that Monica who was our senior, has become an actress. How she managed that I don't know." I was aiming the camera at him while I was talking, and something in his face altered, alerting me.'

'So I asked, "Are you in touch with her?" and he said, "Sort of. I meet her sometimes when I am in Bangalore." Three months later I was reading about the killing in Mumbai.'

Aside from the shock at St Mathias that two of their star students were embroiled in such a scandal, another question—unasked by some; articulated by others—hums through the corridors: What drew the earnest, orderly, go-getter naval officer to the restless, worldly, ambitious actress?

'Everyone at school knew Monica, because she was such a good dancer,' said Vinay, who was three years her junior. 'Even us kids in the primary section.' Emile, who joined the navy after class twelve in 2000, is remembered as the boy marked for a future. 'He was an extraordinary student always stood first in class—excelled at debate, essay writing, general knowledge—and he was so polite and well behaved.' Mary Anthony, who taught him maths and physics at St Mathias was nearly rapturous in describing Emile's accomplishments. 'He won the school many laurels and was a superb athlete as well.'

'Girls from our school used to purposely wander around Emile's house in the hope of bumping into him, but he was choosy and arrogant. Not in a bad sense, but because he was so accomplished at everything he did. A girl's good looks were not enough, he wanted her to have everything, and which is why we were shocked when we came to know that he went after Monica.' Vinay used the phrase 'went after,' implicitly believing it was Emile who wooed her, and not the other way round.

On their first date, Maria told Emile she was meeting him with only marriage in mind. 'If you are looking to flirt or have an affair, go look elsewhere.' Emile had laughed. 'How can you say such things in a first meeting?' They had so far only exchanged a few emails.

'Marriage was nowhere on his mind,' Maria told me. 'But when you behave in a manner of certain expectation, the other person starts responding accordingly.' They met on Orkut where she had liked his pictures, she told me. One of the photographs that Emile posted was a picture of him standing guard in dashing whites behind President A.P.J. Abdul Kalam during his visit to their naval base.

Emile and Maria met in early 2007, when Emile was posted at Vizag and Maria had returned from Mumbai from her first year-long stint in the city, unable to make it in Bollywood. 'I did not care for him much at that first meeting, even though I told him I was meeting with marriage in mind. He'd worn jeans and some khadi shirt, while I am very particular about clothing, and like to dress well.' She said this in that flirty way where criticism is to be read as coded desire.

The verdict in the case was barely some days away and their lawyers were pitching a cut-throat defence inside the courtroom. One morning Maria's lawyer Sharif Shaikh announced in court that his client was a virgin, and there was no question of a relationship with any man, be it Neeraj or Emile. Maria, who had not been consulted before this line of argument, was chagrined, and wanted to know if the court would insist on a medical test. But while Emile grew increasingly terse and businesslike with her, she retreated into submission, her feelings for him evident. 'I have come to know him better in these last three years during our court meetings than I did in our one year of courtship. Given time and space I feel we can work out our relationship.'

After their first date, they met each other only seven or eight times in the year they were together, but fuelled their long-distance romance with extended telephone calls every day. A month before Neeraj's death, Maria told Emile's friend and course mate who had insisted on speaking to her: 'Watch out for me on TV. I am soon going to be in a Balaji serial.'

She had travelled to Mumbai, met Neeraj and auditioned for Draupadi's role in *Mahabharat* on March 16, and in spite of her poor audition believed, or was led to believe, that she stood a good chance of getting the part. She even mentioned Neeraj to Emile's course mate asking if he had heard of him. 'I was quite surprised and told her the only person I knew from TV was Smriti Irani.'

'Emile often worried about her negotiating her way through the film and TV world all alone,' the same course mate said. He agreed to an interview, but service rules prevent him from giving his name. 'Monica had told him that a music director in Bangalore was holding up her dues for some songs that she had recorded with him.'

But Emile's real, if unspoken, concern was Mumbai's infamous casting couch. It was also one of the reasons Emile's conservative parents objected to his relationship with Maria. 'They'd call me up and ask me to tell Emile to stop seeing her, until finally I told them, "You're his parents, you have greater control over him, and if you can't stop him, how can I, a mere friend, do anything? He has set boundaries for me that I cannot breach."'

Once, when Maria was unable to reach Emile, she called his course mate to leave a message and he mentioned the family's fears to her. 'I know the casting couch exists in Mumbai but I don't need to get down to it, my father is well-to-do and influential, and no one can force me,' she had assured him. 'And I got convinced. At least in real life she seemed to be a good actress,' he said. 'Still, I wanted to watch out for Emile so I pressed further: "You're a movie star, you can get any hunk, why settle for Emile, he's just a regular naval officer".' At this, he said Maria became sentimental and told him Emile's profession or his lack of wealth was not important to her. 'I really love him, and you must believe that.' Though the couple was never formally engaged, she always introduced Emile as her fiancé. He was the only man she ever acknowledged to her family as her boyfriend. Like Maria, Emile had never publicly acknowledged a lover—and he too introduced Maria to his friends in the navy as his girlfriend.

When Maria was flying out to the UK to visit Veronica in December 2007, Emile took leave of absence and came to Mumbai to see her off. He took her to the hill station of Lonavla, where he had spent four years at the naval base INS Shivaji acquiring a B.Tech. in mechanical engineering. He also introduced her to one of his closest friends, Lieutenant Jitesh Saini, at Navy Nagar in Mumbai. It was a brief meeting suffused with the formality accorded to a brother officer's spouse or girlfriend, but Emile did pull Jitesh aside to say that he was 'serious about Monica'.

'After one of his interminable phone calls to Monica, I'd asked him: "Are you serious or just having mazaa with the actress?" said the course mate, 'And he told me, "nahin yaar, I really want to marry her."' Maria too reciprocated with serious intent. '"I am a very good dancer, he has two left feet, I sing really well, he can't hold a tune, he can't even paint," she told me with an indulgent smile.'

So what was it that she liked about him? 'For one, he looked my age though his mother thought I looked older than him. He had good etiquette. It's really important to me. For instance, in jail, I can't stand it when people speak to me using tu, tum, or re. I always say, aap is such a beautiful word, use it! I also noticed he wielded a fork and knife very neatly. Manners, discipline, and humbleness are important to me, and he had all of that.'

'I wasn't looking for financial stability, my father had enough money. What I liked about him was that he was from Mysore, his house was a few minutes away from ours, he was a Roman Catholic like us, everyone knew his family. I thought if something did go wrong between us, the families would be there to take care of it. I made sure all the boxes ticked. You know,' and here she paused for a long time, 'my mother had even planned the theme and the colours for our wedding.'

What she had not accounted for was that her reputation from the film world would spill over into the small town of Mysore—and reach Emile's mother. 'When her family sent a proposal in early 2008, Emile's parents had already done a background check on the girl, and decided against the match,' said a relative of Emile's who spoke on the condition of anonymity. The stand-off with the family was a first for Emile. As the model, super-achieving son, he was only ever used to unqualified love and appreciation from his parents. 'They had been extraordinarily protective of Emile,' remembered Vinay. 'As kids, on the rare occasion we got to go to a classmate's home after school, his mother would always take the phone number of that boy and then call his home to find out if Emile had reached, and when he would leave. Whereas most of our mothers couldn't be bothered as long as we got home in the time we said we would.' His father always accompanied him when he went for a swimming class at the pool in the Mysore University campus, and later, when he joined the navy, they would speak to him every day that he was available on base.'

But after he told them about Maria, their daily phone calls were used to pressure him to leave her. Emile would politely hear them out, trying without much success to convince them that she was indeed a suitable girl for him.

'As compared to his personality, the girl was no match for him. If you just look at her you'll know what I am talking about.' Such was the animosity that Emile's relative felt for Maria, that he would not even take her name, referring to her throughout our conversation as 'the girl'.

Exhausted by the abrasive battle with his parents, Emile called his friend Jitesh to complain. 'Ghar pe maan nahin rahein hain' (They are not agreeing at home). Briefly, to ease the pressure, Emile even told his parents that he had broken up with Maria. They believed him until Maria started turning up at the same church as theirs.

'But his mother would snub me every time I made an effort to reach out to them,' said Maria, unable to hide her hurt even after all these years. When she returned from England after visiting Veronica, she got a gift for Emile's mother who refused it, insisting churlishly, 'We have everything we need, why don't you give it to one of your friends?' Maria, who read special prayers at the Basilica at Vailankkani for her and Emile's marriage, says whatever Emile's parents said about her character hurt her family 'badly'.

'Monu, just give me some time, they'll come around,' Emile kept pleading with Maria, while at the same time telling her he could not decide between her and his parents, who remained adamant. 'She's not right for our family, don't talk to her,' they kept insisting, still treating him like a little boy. 'Whenever they called me to talk Emile out of his infatuation,' said his course mate, 'they'd just say one thing. She's not from our world, she will not fit in with our family.'

Unlike the Susairajs, whom he saw as arrivistes from Tamil Nadu, Emile's father, also called Joseph—Jerome Joseph—counted his family, the Mareths, among the old genteel Malayalee Christians of Wayanad where they owned a small coffee plantation. He himself had worked in the junior management of the Bank of Maharashtra's Bhandup branch in Mumbai, but transferred to the more tranquil city of Mysore when his sons began to grow up. The family settled in NR Mohalla, a modest neighbourhood five kilometres from the plush Bannimantap, where Maria lived with her parents and went to school.

Deeply religious, Emile's father was proud of his two sisters who became nuns, one of whom went on to head the highly respected college of Home Science, Nirmala Niketan. His older brother was a brigadier in the Indian Army, while Emile's grandfather had been the postmaster general of Kerala. Following his own voluntary retirement from the Bank of Maharashtra, Jerome Joseph dabbled in shares, selling LIC policies and liaising for those interested in buying or selling property in and around Wayanad. But these were diversions for him. His life's project was his two sons—the younger Nirmal, or Tuttu as he is called at home, pursuing his masters in psychology and criminology at university in Chennai, and Unni, which is Emile's pet name. Even as he was growing up, Jerome Joseph knew that his elder son was exceptional. Beautiful, dutiful, of a serious mien—whatever Unni set his mind to, he excelled at.

'But the person Emile was closest too was his mother. I've often seen him, this full-grown man, this smart naval officer, lying down resting his head in his mother's lap,' his relative said. 'She was too distressed to even visit him in jail for the first couple of years. Instead, she kept exhorting her kin to tell Emile to just, pray, pray, and pray...'

On May 8, 2008, the day after Neeraj's death, Jerome Joseph landed up unexpectedly at the naval base in Kochi. Emile was not yet back from Mumbai, and had not been answering calls for three days. That, and some parental instinct, prompted the surprise visit. 'He was awfully disturbed to know that Emile was not at the base. "Will it not get him into trouble with his superiors?" he kept asking me,' said Emile's course mate.

'When I called Emile in Mumbai to tell him that his father had arrived and what I should say to him, he said, "Just tell him that I have gone to meet Monica."' The next morning when Emile arrived at the base, father and son had a blazing row. 'How could you just leave like that and go to Mumbai? You will lose your career for this girl,' Jerome Joseph screamed with helplessness. 'You know your mother has not been doing well but you are spoiling your life for that girl. She has money, but you, you will lose everything,' he said, unaware how prophetic his words would be. Emile, his son, his thew and sinew, his hope, his lament, stood with his head bowed, that cupid mouth set firmly without offering any defence.

It should have been a happy realization to Jerome Joseph, but it came to him as a shock—his son had become his own man, and he no longer had the right of way with him. Any deference was mere gesture, like those men who hide their cigarettes behind their backs when an elder goes by.

'When Emile told me of his problems at home, I felt a bit bad for his father because Emile is a determined guy and once he'd decided that Monica was the girl for him, then it would be she and no other.' I met another of Emile's friends secretly, away from the naval base in Kochi, and he too spoke on the condition of anonymity, afraid of adverse action from his bosses if his name came out.

When I asked him why he would take such a risk, he said, 'Because he is the guy least heard in your story. Neeraj is the victim, Maria is the actress'—a slight curl of the lip more evocative than his words—'and besides, she has already given a confession before the magistrate putting all the blame on Emile, so where does that leave him? I know he'll not do anything undignified to defend himself.'

This was a theme that came up with everyone I talked to about Emile. Maria had few intimates to speak of, and Neeraj's friends' accounts of him—though fond and warmly spoken—often ended with caveats. It was only from Emile's friends that I got a sense of unconditional loyalty. Maybe it's the years in the navy where they are trained, if need be, to die for a brother officer. A course mate from Emile's division recalls his extraordinary sensitivity. 'While we were at Lonavla, Emile had a very public showdown with one of his peers and things became quite awkward between them until one day the other guy came and apologized to Emile, who was so remorseful that he started to cry.'

After failing to crack the Indian Institute of Technology's joint entrance exam, which he sat for along with Vinay, Emile cleared the Naval Engineers Course in 2000. He was sent to Goa for a six-month orientation where he met his course mates who now defend him. By the time they eventually settled at the INS Shivaji, Lonavla, for the B.Tech., friendships had been forged—especially between the nineteen cadets, Emile included—from the C division.

At Lonavla, Emile, often ribbed as Emily, stood out as a brilliant all-rounder. He was a tri-athlete, achieved good grades with practised ease, did cross-country running, water skiing, and sailing, but saved his best efforts for swimming. 'He would swim up to ten kilometres without a break, often participating in endurance swimming competitions organized at the National Defence Academy at Khadakvasla and winning the blazer,' said the course mate. 'If there was one word to capture Emile's personality, I'd say he was a stud.'

There are two criteria for cadets to get to the next semester. They have to clear tests and get past a gruelling physical exam. 'He managed to do both in the first attempt, every semester. I am making a mention of this because only fifteen per cent of the class manages to do so.' For his accomplishments Emile was chosen to lead his division, an honour known as Appointment. He proved to be an excellent leader and teammate. 'The navy's rules can test the mettle of any man but Emile was always relaxed, he never snitched, and could be trusted even in the weirdest of situations. If there was any issue, it was with his temper.'

Emile, it seems, did not like being crossed. 'If someone did not follow his instructions despite warning, he was capable of grabbing them by the collar and cuffing them.' I was told that while this was not a common thing on the base, it was not entirely unheard of either. Emile's battle with his temper began in his childhood.

'At St Mathias we used to have this game, one of those stupidly cruel games only boys would play, where one person crept up from behind and shut a boy's eyes while the rest just piled on to him, hitting and kicking,' recalled Vinay. 'It was a good way to rag those we didn't like. Though Emile was my closest friend, a whole group of boys once convinced me to shut Emile's eyes as he returned from a water break. His fury when I did so was unbelievable. Even as I held him I could feel his body shivering with the force of his anger. Okay, so you're with them, he told me freeing himself in one heave; he was such a strong boy that instead of the others beating him it was he who lashed out at them. Within minutes those boys had all fled and I was left writhing in pain for he had kicked me also in the bargain. His anger that day was terrifying. After that episode, though we patched up soon after, I was always wary of provoking him. I was a little afraid of him, I guess.'

Another time, a social science teacher they disliked—'she was not very bright and we let her know that'—singled out the two boys in front of the class and assigned them a project on China. 'It was out of the syllabus and out of our league. We were given some ridiculous deadline of a day or two to complete it and I was sure we would fail, but Emile, angry and humiliated at being singled out, dragged me to the Mysore Central Library. I'd never ever been there and we spent hours poring over books on China. Then through his father, he spoke to someone who knew all about the country. The teacher was stumped when we submitted the project on time. She tried to regain ground by saying she would be asking us questions, but Emile who could be polite and insolent at the same time shot back, "Miss, read the project and you will have no question that has not already been answered."'

His friends in the navy call him a 'polished guy, but one who could not bear to be fingered'. Strains of this were already apparent in his adolescence. When Emile was finishing high school at Marimala Pass—after having completed his middle school at St Mathias—recounts another classmate, there was a very popular boy who was contesting for class representative. 'For some reason he and Emile got into a scrap. Almost at the last moment, when this boy's victory seemed certain, Emile propped up another candidate against him, a complete underdog, and championed his case so persuasively that the guy won, beating the favourite by one vote.'

Though the navy was a perfect fit for his temperament, if not necessarily his temper, it could not quite contain Emile's ambition. He studied to be an aircraft engineer; at the time of his arrest he was a specialist in the maintenance of the Russian aircraft Ilyushin at the Naval Institute of Aeronautical Technology in Kochi. But his heart was set on becoming a marine commando.

When he heard of a vacancy he trained strenuously for months to qualify, but was not selected. The navy, combating a shortage of trained technical staff and having spent considerably on his engineering education, was unwilling to have him move streams, according to his friends. Emile himself told Vinay when he last met him in the coffee shop that he was really depressed when they turned him down and it had taken him two months to emerge from that low. He grew close to Maria during this time, and the two of them even made desperate plans for Emile to quit the navy after his engineering so they could go live abroad.

Though he couldn't become a Marco—they were the first line of defence when terrorists laid siege on the Taj Mahal Hotel in Mumbai on 26/11 before the National Security Guards flew in—Emile independently took the gruelling divers' course which was part of the commandos' training programme. Of the thirty-odd applicants from all over the country only five or six made the final cut. Emile was one of them. 'In the navy, divers are looked upon as special people, as someone who is tougher than the rest,' admitted one of Emile's senior officers. The course calls for immense physical courage, and a level of fitness far higher than in a regular navy man. The divers are trained to deal with different situations under water—from combat to rescue ops. 'They push you to extreme limits,' said one of Emile's admiring course mates.

Willingdon Island in Kochi, where Emile was posted at the time of his arrest, is a man-made legacy of the British. The INS Garuda sprawls in the middle of it, offering an idyll full of old-world courtesies, exquisitely manicured flower beds and quaint cottages. Agile young officers wake up at dawn for the morning drill before going to class to study, followed by gym or basketball. The evening's excitements can entail a trip into Kochi town for a few beers, watching the lambent twilight, or a film maybe. It is also a man's world, with little role for women other than maintaining house or participating in the occasional navy social.

Emile and his roommate Lieutenant Vasanth often spent their evenings surreptitiously cooking in their room, watching films like *The Da Vinci Code* and *American Pie* on Emile's laptop, or simply reading. Emile read voraciously, especially favouring books on Christianity. Pope Joseph Ratzinger's *Jesus of Nazareth* was a particular favourite. When not reading or watching films, the young men relieved the tedium of the evening watching the crime show *Sansani* on Aaj Tak. 'It is so melodramatic, so ridiculous that it often afforded us a good laugh. . . I wasn't to know that one day I'd see Emile featuring on the same show,' Vasanth told the police.

This was more or less Emile's life from the time he finished school, stepping out of the security of home straight into another cocooned environment. The regimentation, the elaborate formalities, the puff and pageantry, left him utterly unprepared for the fluid mess of relationships with complex women. 'He was aware that women appreciated him, but while he could have—I've seen girls hovering around him—he never took advantage of them,' said a friend.

Emile found himself undone by Maria's petite charms, her maternal instincts, and reassembled by her feminine playfulness and her seeming vulnerability. 'She stood by me when I was going through a low phase,' he once told me from jail, referring to the time when he failed to get into the commando course. The enforced distance also meant their exposure to one another was selective; the few times they came together each presented their best selves for the delectation of the other.

In March 2008, a month or so before she went back to Mumbai, Maria went to Kochi to spend a few days with Emile. It was to be their last holiday. During the trip, he introduced her to his course mates. 'I saw her, and said to myself—is this one a heroine! Then I thought, maybe. . . Kannada films,' one of them jested. Maria had evoked a similar reaction in Neeraj's friends, who had also been underwhelmed by her looks. I remember his roommate Haresh Sondarva looking at Maria's smiling photograph in the newspapers, a month or so after the killing, and saying dismissively, 'Pata nahin kaun si jawaani ki photo hai' (It's a photograph from her bygone youth).

Regardless, Emile was besotted.

He talked with Maria daily, keeping her appraised of every bit of his day down to what meals he had had, and he expected the same detailed accounts from her. Though they spoke in Kannada, a course mate said he often caught Emile asking her in English, 'Where are you, who are you with?'

'Sometimes, I could make out from his tone of voice that they were having a fight over her whereabouts. He was so possessive about her.'

A senior police officer who was part of the investigation into Neeraj's disappearance revealed that Emile did not like the implications of Maria being an actress—he did not even want his course mates to see her films. 'I remember asking him if he kept any DVDs of Monica's films and him refusing curtly. I could tell he did not want to talk about those movies,' recalled one of his navy friends. And yet, says the police officer, Emile was taken up with the idea of having a glamorous woman as his girlfriend—though it seemed he had little idea of her romantic history.

But within a year of their meeting, this possessiveness coupled with his inability to offer her a firm commitment began to undermine their relationship. The Maria who came to Mumbai in April 2008 was a different creature from the woman who had arrived three years before. She had lost weight dramatically, shrinking to mousy proportions, her pronounced dark circles caused comment, and her ambition had the edge of desperation. The woman whom Kiran described as 'no go-getter' now clung to Neeraj's casual promises as if to a lifeline, seeing highways to glory in the feeble trails he offered.

And what of Emile caught between his parents implacable 'no', and his lover's soft persistence? Every strenuous objection his parents made added to Maria's appeal, and also to Emile's guilt and feelings of obligation towards her. After she arrived in Mumbai on April 29, 2008, Maria started to bring Neeraj into their conversation with disturbing frequency.

Past evidence suggests a pattern in Maria's behaviour, but unlike her openness with her Bangalore boyfriend, Pavan Kumar, she did not disclose to Emile the extent of her involvement with Neeraj, for she desperately wanted a marriage with him. But the merest hint of another man was enough to create malignant doubt. On the night of

May 6, when he called Maria, Emile heard Neeraj's voice in the background. It was well past 11 pm, early hours in Mumbai but extremely late for sleepy Kochi. What was Neeraj doing in Maria's flat at that hour, he demanded to know. Maria had just moved into the new flat at Dheeraj Solitaire that morning and she had called Neeraj over to help her shift, she told him. As the lovers bickered, Maria told Emile her phone battery was dying, and asked him to call her on Neeraj's number. The two men spoke. One, a glib flirt; the other, a conservative, possessive man with an enormous sense of propriety and a temper.

'He wants to know what I'm doing here,' Neeraj hollered in the background when Emile was speaking to Maria a few minutes later. 'What kind of a fiancé is he when his girlfriend needs another man to be with her?'

We will never know if these were words spoken in jest, a burst of misplaced machismo, or sheer viciousness. We'll never know, but they were a catalyst to the events of the next morning.

'I had gone to a party organized by my juniors while Emile had been talking to Monica. He was pacing constantly and he was on the hands-free. At 11.30 pm when I got back to the room I saw Emile in a state of extreme agitation,' Emile's roommate, Lieutenant Vasanth Kumar, told the police, recalling the events of that night. 'He demanded the keys to my motorcycle, saying that he had to leave for the airport and that he would bring the bike back upon his return.' In his state of upset he entirely disregarded Vasanth's warning about breach of discipline. 'It's a matter of life and death,' he said implacably, determined to leave. 'My ticket has been bought.'

'I could see Emile was shaking even as he spoke to me, asking for the keys,' Lieutenant Vasanth recorded in his statement to the police. It was the same body language that had left a younger Vinay fearful of him, and a whole batch of St Mathias classmates battered and bruised. Convinced that Emile would have an accident if he drove in this agitated state, Vasanth offered to drop him to the airport for his flight. Emile packed a bag and the two friends set off at midnight without informing anyone at the base. En route, Emile got another call from Maria. 'He got off the bike and walked some distance away so I could not hear anything of their conversation.'

As for Neeraj, he spoke to his friend, the television actress Barsha Chatterjee at 1.30 am, promising to meet her for breakfast at seven in the morning. It was his last recorded call, after which he put away his mobile in the other room, and turned his attention to Maria.

Book II

Oshiwara—Three Characters in Search of a Film

4

Ekta Kapoor

'The young, especially those from small towns and middle class families, like Neeraj, join because they want quick money, they want expression—their names and faces on TV.'

—Ekta Kapoor

Ekta Kapoor walked into the meeting late, and within ten seconds, like a tearaway bully on the beach, she dismantled all the castles the others had been building. 'I want *Crash*,' she said, referring to Paul Haggis's multiple-Oscar winning film.

The meeting had been convened to discuss her newest project, a movie 'inspired' by Neeraj Grover's killing. Ten films, Ekta informed everyone, had already been announced on the subject. Since Neeraj was a Balaji product and Maria had come to Mumbai aspiring to work with Ekta, it only made logical sense that they should stake ownership.

'If there has to be a film on the TV industry then why shouldn't we be the ones making the story?'

Except, at this point, there was no story.

The executives of Balaji's fledgling film division, and the actor Rohit Roy, who had been signed on to direct his first full-length feature film, were in a massive conference room, brainstorming. 'I have the opening sequence all ready in my head—it begins with a woman's audition tape running. . .' Rohit said to the young assistant who had joined the company two days ago; the assistant looked suitably impressed. Someone suggested a Madhur Bhandarkar-style voyeuristic drama, while another executive came up with the idea of an 'intense love story'. The consensus was veering in that direction when *Crash* landed.

'It blew my mind,' Ekta said. 'Let's also have the plot set over one night featuring several characters and their stories. . . Your budget,' she said, turning towards Rohit, who was beginning to lose some of his good cheer, 'would be Rs two to three crore.'

I met Ekta, India's most successful television producer—and an astute mind—to get an insider's perspective on the world that Neeraj and Maria aspired to. At which she suggested I sit in on her meetings to see how she works and creates.

In the US, a single episode of a television show like *Sex and the City* or *The Wire* costs more than the budget she was offering Rohit for his film. But television in India works on simple volume—the more episodes you produce the more money you make. 'It's not amazing talent that makes me special,' Ekta explained without any hint of self-deprecation, 'but the sheer volume of work I have done.' In its fourteen years, her company has produced over seventy shows, which have defined Indian television. Her approach to movies is similar. 'I'd like to produce quickies made on a tight budget.'

The quick turnover demands a constant feed of actors, technicians, and scriptwriters, making Balaji Telefilms one of the largest employers in Bollywood. 'Every day about a hundred people come to us looking for jobs. I know, because I have to deal with them.' Like Muammar Gaddafi's battalion of women bodyguards, a brisk bevy of bejewelled, tilak-sporting women that included a writer, a head of production, and an assistant, insulate Ekta from the pressures of her own celebrity status. Tanushree Dasgupta, who has been with her for nine years, is at their head.

When Ekta, famously and publicly devout, goes jogging every Tuesday from Mahim to Siddhivinayak Temple at Prabhadevi, she is often waylaid by people on the road wanting roles for themselves, their children; she hands them Tanushree's number. Others get in touch with acquaintances working at Balaji Telefilms while trying for a break, as Maria Susairaj did. Maria befriended Balaji employee Jyoti Jhanavi on Orkut, who in turn introduced her to Neeraj, who was in charge of auditions there. Most recently, Ekta's Facebook account had been overrun with pictures of young men baring their six-packs. 'They think that's their show-reel,' she said, quite tickled.

Last year, a twenty-eight-year-old aspiring scriptwriter from Naini, Uttar Pradesh, Akshay Shivam Shukla, having exhausted all avenues of meeting the Boss Lady, came up with a most ingenuous plan. On August 4, the day of Shravan Puja, he infiltrated the Balaji Telefilms office disguised as a priest.

Unfortunately for him, the staff soon realized that instead of mantras, Panditji was mumbling mumbo-jumbo. Shukla was pulled aside, questioned, and thrown out. In protest, he spent the night outside Balaji House, and when morning came he tried to immolate himself with a litre and a half of kerosene. The watchmen, desperate to douse the flames, pushed him into the open sewer that runs alongside the building. Cops were called in, a case was registered, and Shukla—finally deterred from his mission to meet Ekta—was admitted to Cooper Hospital.

'Eighty per cent of people in TV today have gone through Balaji,' she told me, with pride. 'The young, especially those from small towns and middle class families, like Neeraj, join because they want quick money, they want a platform to express themselves, to see their names and faces on TV. In their hometowns, TV is the primary source of entertainment, and to have their families see their name and face on TV is a big power trip.'

Her own creative head, Vikas Gupta, was a loose-limbed, floppy-haired twenty-one-year-old from Uttarakhand who leapfrogged up the hierarchy one evening when he saw Ekta struggling to figure out what had gone wrong with one of her episodes. 'My mother would not buy the logic of the lead character,' he told her casually.

'On instinct,' she said snapping her fingers, 'I decided to make him Balaji's creative head. It's a big job, and I've made him sign a tough contract, but he understands the audience consists of women like his mother. Also, I liked his attitude.'

That was what had also first brought Neeraj to her attention. As she waited for her private lift to take her up to her fifth floor office, one of the aspirants hanging around on the ground floor saw Ekta and flicked an impertinent salute. 'It was a really arrogant gesture, but I liked it,' she said, letting me into the secret of how she creates stars. 'There are only two things we look for in our lead actors: the man should have attitude, and the woman should look innocent. Between you and me,' she said with a wink, 'virginal.' This has led to some peculiar casting problems—'It's become difficult to find young urban women who meet this criterion.' Ekta bypassed this problem by casting schoolgirls. Her youngest heroine has been a sixteen-year-old.

As television boomed into a Rs 27,000 crore industry in just over ten years, Oshiwara transformed from the dump Ekta first came to in 2000 into one of Mumbai's most fashionable neighbourhoods. Young television stars and technicians, who spent upwards of twelve hours a day in near-squalid studios at Goregaon, Saki Naka, and Malad, going weeks without a break, invested heavily in plush homes here. The skyline is dotted with Singapore-style condominiums with hard-to-pronounce French-sounding names. (The illusion of a First World lifestyle is reinforced with easy access to fancy cold cuts, cheese and wines, the latest Almodovar DVD, and 24/7 air-conditioned houses. This lasts only until one steps outside, and is rudely brought down to potholed earth.) Real estate expansion has been matched by a thriving nightlife, forcing even frou-frou South Mumbai restaurateurs like Rahul Akerkar, the owner of Indigo, to open branches here.

The idea and attitude of Oshiwara now pushes beyond the reclaimed marsh. It is in the vanity of little-known designers housed in glass-plated buildings announcing their genius tersely, like Giorgio Armani, or Jimmy Choo, and without a smidgen of irony: Rahul Agasti, Turakhia Dhaval, Roopa Vora, Babita Malkani.

It is implicit in the flashy EMI-driven lifestyle prevalent here. But most of all it lies, said Jaideep Sahni, in the 'severe ambition' that crackles in the air. His is the classic story of the outsider who made it big in Mumbai. The forty-one-year-old from Delhi is the most sought after scriptwriter in the film industry. 'Just sit at the Yaari Road Barista for half an hour and you will know what it's about. The atmosphere is electric,' he said referring to another coffee shop not far from where Neeraj and his friends hung out each evening. 'Those men and women who look like Conan or Barbie behave as if they are out not for a cup of coffee, but for a screen test. Everything is about getting face time with the right people,' said the writer of hit films like *Company, Bunty Aur Babli, Khosla Ka Ghosla,* and *Chak De.*

Jaideep himself is often accosted at film premieres, where a glass wall cuts the Bollywood hierarchy off from the hoi polloi. Such is the premium on these opening nights that cinema chains like PVR have introduced the idea of 'paid premiere' tickets. 'A well-dressed stranger will persistently catch your eye and since it would be rude to not respond, and one may be unsure of having met them, you go across. That's all they need. After small talk about how they admire your work, or similar fawning attentiveness, they'll follow you back into the enclosure, past the usher, as if that's their natural destination.' He laughed half-admiringly. 'Once in, the person will drop you to go mingle with other directors and producers. Mission accomplished.'

'Every nation has a defining characteristic. If it is confidence for the American, for the Australian it's his appetite for fun. In India, what defines us is striving,' Rajesh Kamat told me. A Mumbai boy, Rajesh was the CEO of Viacom 18, the company that owns the entertainment channel Colors, at the age of thirty-seven. He has left that job since we last spoke. Colors had raced to the top of the Television Rating Point (TRP) chart within a year of its launch, forcing others, including Ekta, to modify their formula. 'It's our striving for a better life, a better lifestyle. There is, even in these tough times, a disproportionate amount of money to be made in TV, which is why it's so seductive for the young.'

Having worked previously with Endemol, a Dutch company that licenses reality show formats—they produced two of the biggest shows on Colors, *Fear Factor* and *Big Boss 2*—Rajesh has closely watched this young workforce turn around the country's television habits—television's eternal saas–bahu sagas ceding ground to starlet Dolly Bindra getting foul-mouthed on camera.

Over the course of an interview that stretched past midnight, Ekta who is now routinely counted among India's wealthiest women, recounted how she started her own career as an eighteen-year-old producer. 'I was in class twelve when my parents shifted from Bandra to their bungalow in Juhu, which I hated. I'd run away to Bandra every day to hang out at the Otters' Club with my friends Anupam and Parvin Dabas, who went on to become an actor, and to walk around Joggers' Park with Aunty Neetu [Singh-Kapoor].'

Additionally, three days of the week were scheduled for partying, which caught the attention of the ever-vigilant *Stardust*. 'I was just excited about doing nothing. I didn't do drugs, I didn't smoke, I rarely drank, but *Stardust* ran a piece saying Jeetendra's daughter was running wild.' Her father, a man of modest and conservative upbringing—his family ran a small business selling artificial jewellery before he went on to become a big star, was appalled. 'He couldn't understand why I needed to be out of the house every second day... Not long after I turned eighteen he came into my room one evening and gave me an ultimatum—either I start working, or get married.'

Ekta grew up watching endless hours of television and devouring tubs of ice cream while her father was busy shooting three shifts a day, and her mother stayed away either travelling with him or at kitty parties. She decided to make television serials. 'I loved TV, it gave me great joy.' Her friend Ratna Rajiah wrote a plot outline, which her cousin Gattu (better known as Abhishek Kapoor, the director of the Farhan Akhtar starrer *Rock On*) would direct. 'Our pilot was called *Jeans 'n' Josh* and I must confess that the title was the only colourful thing about it; the serial was a grim look at things like peer pressure, AIDS, bisexuality, parental hypocrisy. We wanted to be dark and meaningful,' she said, letting out an ironic little giggle. 'It was our equivalent of a Madhur Bhandarkar movie, and both Gattu and I were very proud of it. But when we showed it to Ravina Raj Kohli at Star TV, she took one look at it and dismissed us, saying no channel would commission something so dark, and which dealt with suicide and all. "Give me something happy and family oriented," she said. We were crushed. I remember getting out of the Star office and shaking my head to Gattu: "What's the world come to, I say!"'

But she imbibed Ravina Raj Kohli's instructions well. 'I am not saying we are ashamed of what we do. . . We did create *Kyunki, Kanyadan, Kavyanjali, Kasautti* which have been about the urban middle class, but you are not my audience. You can go home and see *Desperate Housewives* just like I do.'

Her serials are a volatile mix of traditional Indian motifs, often featuring joint families with all their stereotypes, clashing modern values, and are as formulaic as a Bollywood film. When Peter Chernin, then COO of Rupert Murdoch's News Corp (which owns Star TV in India), came to Ekta's home for a meal he asked her what was wrong with one of their new launches, and why it wasn't doing well. 'Even then I told him that his new channel was trying to be a niche channel, and that could never be profitable in India.'

A few years after this well-meaning advice, Star TV terminated their decade-long exclusive partnership with Ekta, axed three of her daily soaps, and divested their 25.99 per cent share in her company. Balaji Telefilms' stock went into a tailspin, sparking a shiver of excitement among Bollywood's obituary writers.

We met again on the day her company lost its arbitration case against Star TV. She had just emerged from a marathon meeting with her creative team, but was still smarting from the judgment. 'I gave Star the best eight, nine years of my life, I took them at face value, but they f***** me over. . .'

'Then again,' she lowered her pitch by a notch or two, 'my Rahu mahadasha has begun, and I've been told my secret enemies will start to surface.'

I asked with curiosity: 'For how long will the mahadasha go on?'

'Eighteen years, man!'

Early propagators of astrology, the Babylonians and the Mayans would read chicken liver for as many as six thousand warning signs. The greater the fear of uncertainty, and the less assurance there is of certitude, leaves the diviner and the follower to try every possible form of propitiation.

Such was the case with Ekta, who wore a stone on every finger, even two on some. Over the many doors of the seven-storeyed Balaji House, horseshoes, clutches of fresh neon-green chillies and lemon are tied along with coconuts wrapped in an auspicious red, dangling like the breasts of a baboon. On Ekta's fifth floor domain as well as at her Juhu house the Gayatri mantra, sung in a fast-paced tinny-voice, as if on a worn-out tape, plays round the clock working like a force field against any possible evil eyes.

A former employee clued me in, 'Whenever you meet her, take a close look at her shoes.' The woman who could easily afford the latest Manolos and Louboutins only ever wore a pair of worn-out platform slip-ons, straps in tatters, with the clunky rubber heels roughened. 'She considers them her lucky shoes and won't trade them for another pair.'

Not long after hearing this, I read an interview with Ekta in *Hindustan Times* in which, speaking about her shows on Colors, Ekta said her association with the channel would be fruitful, she knew, because when it's creative head first called she'd been in a puja, and as soon as their conversation ended a flower dropped from the head of the idol. It was, Ekta said, a divine seal of approval.

~

I sat in on one of her meetings, hoping to catch some of the action—it was rumoured that in fits of rage she threw slippers (the lucky ones?) at errant employees; but while I was there, she remained regrettably in control.

Of the ten serials that are in production at any given time, Ekta only looks after three—the rest are taken care of by associates—but she decides the look and casting for each of the shows. 'I remember we shortlisted a girl for our serial *Kasturi*, but when I came back from out of town and saw the hoardings, I realized her face did not reflect the innocence demanded by the character. Overnight the hoardings were brought down, a fake story about how pressure had made the actress ill was circulated in the media, and a new girl was found.'

Ekta talked from behind a presidential-size desk as Vikas showed her auditions of aspirants—this is what Neeraj Grover used to do at Balaji Telefilms. Also present were seven or eight young women, all under thirty. Ekta stared hard at the computer screen, and pressed the enter key with the speed and concentration of a tabla player beating a riff on the dagga. Though the air conditioner remote was lying next to her, she passed it to one of the girls every few minutes: 'On karo... ab off karo. Switch it on... ab off...'

Mothers, sisters—'kindly faces', buas and sisters-in-law—'nice bitchy faces' were swiftly cast before trouble erupted. 'Where's the father? The Marathi actor I asked you guys to locate, the one who looks like an older Ajay Devgn?' There was a shuffle of confusion, and Vikas pressed ahead trying to show her other options, but she refused to be appeased.

'WHERE IS THE GUY I WANT?'

The entire group involuntarily moved back a step. Was I about to witness a famous Ekta blowout? Instead, she abruptly switched her tone and turned to me. 'I got the idea for the film on Neeraj from something you said. General wisdom is that creative directors like him have no clout, they merely audition...but I got thinking, and it struck me that I get to see only what they choose to show me. They actually have the power to make or break someone's career. If my staff shows me the photograph of an actor just as I am leaving for home, getting into the car, ninety per cent chances are I'll say okay. That's the time I am exhausted and not as hawk-eyed... This power and what they choose to do with it is what I want to explore in the film.'

She then got up, and with a gesture intended to be theatrical, pulled me into the corridor. 'If you're doing a book on Neeraj Grover, you must speak to Smita Patil,' she said sotto voce. 'She's a spook, man!'

Though Neeraj had quit working for Ekta Kapoor several months earlier, when he went missing Ekta got one of her colleagues to contact a clairvoyant for his whereabouts. It was a far more reliable source of information for her than any detective could offer. 'I knew Neeraj was dead even before the police announced it. This woman had told us that his girlfriend, along with two other men, had killed him, and she also gave details of where his body could be found.'

Two days later she texted me the mobile number of her clairvoyant, Smita Patil.

The phone beeped, and Narendra Chanchal's '*Chalo bulawaa aaya hai, maata ne bulaya hai*'...rang in my ear. Mid-crescendo, Smita Patil cut him short and answered the phone. She had been a Goregaon girl who got her degree in textile designing from Sophia Polytechnic, and married an assistant geologist in ONGC. For several years she taught art in various schools, all the while nursing political ambitions. In 1999 she was jailed during a political agitation, and was featured in the *Bombay Times* as 'Star of the Week'.

A devotee of Durga from her early days, she did the punishing nine-day nirjala vrat every Navratri to invoke the goddess. 'People started making fun of my bhakti so I prayed hard to Mata Rani, saying she needed to manifest herself and save me from such humiliation. In 2005, Mata Rani housed herself in my body and she has stayed on since, constantly showing her chamatkar.'

Every Tuesday at her home, which is right next to a teeming mall at Bhayander, she holds a durbar where Mata Rani—and here Smita Patil referred to herself in the third person—gives darshan seated on her high chair, doling out individual benedictions after the prayers. From healing invalids to blessing the childless, Mata Rani's bounty, she says, knows no limit.

'In May last year one of my bhakts, a girl called Rasika, came in with her boyfriend Kushal who works at Balaji, he wanted to know the whereabouts of his friend Neeraj. I took one look at Neeraj's picture and said, "The boy is no more, his girlfriend and two men are responsible, and the body can be found near water." Kushal told me no one would kidnap Neeraj, and that he didn't think that's what had happened. So I closed my eyes again and told him that Mata Rani had spoken and that the girlfriend should be taken to the CBI and she would confess.'

'This Kushal called me one evening some days later and said, "Mata Rani, please switch on the TV. Whatever you said has come true."' She has guided several celebrities in addition to Ekta, even telling a powerful Shiv Sena politician that he was going to die soon.

And, did he? It was impossible to resist the question.

'Within three days of my informing him this, he had an accident and died.'

But it's not easy being Mata Rani, taking care of bhoot-balaayein, and dialoguing with the spirits. 'If it's a shaitani shakti I have to counter, I suffer tremendously, my feet get crooked, I start yelling and then my body starts to get heavier and heavier. Mata Rani needs to be in a pure environment and you can imagine what that means in a filthy city like Mumbai... It's difficult to walk on roads, travel by train, I can't clean my house, wash utensils, normal life is not possible with Mata Rani constantly living in my body. The family life is affected too.' But her children, one of whom studies aeronautical engineering in Nashik while the other is in class XI, have come to accept the new presence in their mother's life.

'My dream is to serve the people and have a temple built in Mata Rani's name at my residence, for that's where her shrine stood four hundred years ago, and which was later buried under rubble. Mata Rani needs to be brought out from under the earth and allowed to breathe.'

Superstitions and clinging to totems sit oddly with the woman I've been interviewing. Ekta is bright, humorous, and in possession of a combative streak. I mentioned this to a television insider who has dealt closely with Balaji Telefilms, and who agreed to speak provided I kept his identity concealed. 'To understand the Ekta phenomenon,' he said chuckling quietly, 'you must also know the father and the mother. Brand Ekta is the three of them operating as a unit.'

Shobha Kapoor, a former flight attendant, is the canny dowager whose business deals are as sharp as her diamonds. Her rough cuts are offset by Ekta's father. Jeetendra was India's original dancing star who, when thirty was thought of as middle age, famously endorsed a brand of virility capsules called 'Thirty Plus'. 'Jeetendra is charm and gentleness personified,' my informer explained.

The final member of the troika is Ekta, the unpredictable, superstitious diva with a famous temper, who creates amidst chaos. 'The mother will play hardball with a channel in the morning, but blame Ekta's working style when executives complain of schedules going awry or tapes coming in late. If the channel ever suggests dropping a Balaji show that may be faring poorly, Jeetendra will take the executives out for a drink by the evening and get emotional and apologetic, saying: "You know just how eccentric Ekta is, all the shows are like her babies, I understand your problem but if you drop one of the shows, she may get upset, that in turn may affect her creativity, and impact the rest of the serials on the channel..."' The insider laughed, putting aside his masala chai. 'It's a brilliant strategy.'

I got the drift of her mercurial style one evening when she called me over to her house. 'I'll be relaxed there and we can chat at leisure.' But the meeting was rescheduled four times before she sent a message saying that she would definitely be home by 11 pm. These days Amitabh Bachchan might woefully blog about waterlogging at his house each time it rains heavily, but until recently, the Juhu Vile-Parle Development Scheme was one of the most elegant addresses in Mumbai. A generation of movie stars—

Dharmendra, Amitabh Bachchan, Rakesh Roshan, Shatrughan Sinha, and Hema Malini—live in plush fenced-off bungalows there. A few years ago, when Hema Malini decided to reconstruct her home, she looked around for a temporary apartment in the vicinity—but quickly dropped the idea when she discovered she was expected to share the elevator with the other residents of the building.

Her contemporary, and one-time suitor, Jeetendra has a house which stands out in the neighbourhood as one of the largest. It also resembles a Jain temple, built as it is in blinding-white marble. But the presiding deity was not in.

Instead, I was ushered in with my *Mumbai Mirror* colleague Vickey Lalwani into a high-ceilinged room so large that it looked unused. In a far corner, Ekta's photographs in various poses lined the shelf—she has a sweet face and a lovely smile, but the hauteur in the eyes is unmistakable. A sprawling chandelier hung over a bare dining table; Grecian-style pillars and a forlorn-looking marble nymph added to the mausoleum-like feel. The same tinny-voiced Gayatri mantra was playing here too, though there didn't seem to be a soul around. As the minutes elapsed, Vickey and I silently stared at Ekta's black pug desperately humping a velvet sofa cushion.

Suddenly, Jeetendra glided noiselessly into the room, looking dressed for a night out. After solicitous small talk he called out, conjuring a flurry of liveried attendants, as he did Ekta who arrived within seconds. It was past midnight, but she had been out jogging. 'The three most important things in my day are: exercise, prayer, meetings, in that order of priority.' She would jog anywhere, any time, which explained her perennial uniform of T-shirts and track pants. Very different from her growing-up years, when she favoured hip clothing.

'I was 84 kilos when I was eighteen, that's the heaviest I've ever been. That happened because when I'd be at home, I would do nothing but sit in front of the TV or talk to my friends on the phone, and eat tubs of ice cream. That too full cream—there were none of the 96 percent fat-free gelatos in those days.' She laughed. 'One of the reasons I partied so hard was to get slim. It was my way of keeping away from junk. I wanted to get into "fashionable" clothes,' she rolls her eyes and makes the quote sign, 'dance like crazy, and just hang. By the time I was twenty, I was drinking hot water twenty times a day and my weight had come down to 51 kilos.'

That must have made her happy.

'I can't say about that but I do know I looked ill. I remember my friend, the former actress Neelam, was hospitalized with meningitis; when I went to see her at the hospital her mother was berating her for not eating properly, and then she whipped around to stare at me and said, "You're falling sick next."'

The partying and the skimpy clothes, Ekta said, were a passing phase. Recently, she tried to stop her friend's sixteen-year-old daughter from going off with a television actor after a late night party, and was snubbed for her efforts. 'The young these days are so at ease with their sexuality, and they know what they want in life. They have the drive and the ambition, but I find many of them are so happy with their limited forty-thousand-rupee-a-month lifestyle that they will not work harder to get into the one-lakh-rupee bracket. They need to inculcate the value of hard work.'

Her own strong work ethic and her faith guide her life. Apart from visiting Siddhivinayak Temple every Tuesday, a Shani temple every Saturday, and the Tirupati Balaji temple before launching a show, Ekta said she needed to pray for 'just seven minutes' every day.

Ekta puts in sixteen hours a day—her friend, the Bollywood scriptwriter Mushtaq Shaikh, is writing a book on her called *Holidays Not Allowed*—working through the night, and very often clearing an episode that's scheduled for telecast later that evening at 4 am. When Balaji Telefilms became a public listed company, the joke in the Star TV office was that the risk factor in the share prospectus should mention 'Possibility of Ekta getting married'. Neeraj, who often complained to his roommate Haresh Sondarva about the 'inhuman working conditions at Balaji', and fretted about the long and irregular hours, nonetheless greatly admired Ekta's drive and success.

'I have no family time,' she admitted. Four years ago she built herself a multi-storey bungalow a few hundred metres away from her parents' home. 'I wanted to know what it was like to live by myself.' She shifted into the house with three household helpers, but didn't last beyond a few days. 'It was beautiful, but awfully quiet. . . Here, I know that I have my space but also the knowledge that my parents are floating about somewhere.'

At thirty-six, she is in a 'happy space: I have satisfying work, friends, my own time, I lead a cocooned life.' But things at Balaji have been getting worrisome. News came in that their ambitious show *Mahabharat* on 9X channel (for which Maria had auditioned) would go off the air mid-narrative. The expensive period sets erected cannot be used for any other show, and the money owed to them is unlikely to be paid.

Elsewhere, reality TV shows were flourishing, contributing about 25 percent of the total programming. During a trip to Mysore I met Maria Susairaj's journalism teacher Shabana Mansoor, who has since quit teaching to pursue research on the 'Priming Effect of Television on Young Female Adults'. The research was inspired by a train conversation with a young woman who said she would never want to marry a man whose mother was alive. She had been convinced that mothers-in-law were terrible creatures after growing up on a staple of Ekta Kapoor's trademark 'K'-serials. 'But when I went for my fieldwork I found that most young women now watch the soaps mainly for fashion and interior tips, and their real interest lies elsewhere.' In the villages of Kerala and Karnataka, Shabana was repeatedly asked why she had omitted asking questions about *Roadies* and *Splitsvilla*, the two most popular reality shows on television.

Balaji had been unable to cash in on this brash new phenomenon, still stuck with heavy duty drama. But Ekta had a plan to expand her business, which was soon revealed. As a first step she made up with Star TV, producing new shows for them. After parting ways with her mamaji, Shobha Kapoor's brother and the well-known film distributor Ramesh Sippy, Ekta became firmly in charge of the family's film business. A new CEO was hired, and five films had already been green lit. Three of these were based on real-life incidents, trying for a touch of realism that Ekta could not bring to her television programmes. The film on Neeraj Grover's death never got made, though Ekta produced one of the most celebrated movies of 2009, *Love, Sex Aur Dhoka,* an edgy triptych about sexual betrayal, cinematic aspirations, and parental disapproval—themes that deeply resonated with Neeraj's killing.

But none of the stress from the dwindling bottom line was evident at the party the day after Diwali. It was the annual card fixture the Kapoors hosted to celebrate the festival. Invites had been texted that morning, but it was expected to be a full house. At 1 am the road leading to Ekta's house was crammed with gleaming Mercedes and Beemers. In that darkened lane, Ekta's bungalow was lit up like a piece of jewellery. The lift inside the house carried us to the third floor, and into a hall marked by its quietness. On a cluster of large round tables, Jeetendra, Rakesh Roshan, Sunita Menon, Sawan Kumar Tak, and Manish Malhotra were playing cards with serious intent.

Nobody looked up as other guests walked in and went past. The only sound was the clink of ice in the glasses of single malt and the rueful phew! of a substantial loss. In the adjoining hall, dominated by a stunning chandelier that descended from a dome at least fifty feet high, the scene resembled a Las Vegas casino more than a Mumbai house party. Certainly the décor bore out the excesses of Las

Vegas. The room I was in favoured the ladies—Rakesh Roshan's wife Pinky, Karan Johar's mother Hiroo, Dimple Kapadia (stunning in green), and the actor Akashdeep were dealing with wads of thousand and five hundred rupee notes. Currency was spread out like a tablecloth.

A sudden shriek from the corner of the room had the others rushing over—Dimple had won her first big hand—Rs 50,000. The Juhu film aristocracy was out to play.

I spotted the now-familiar faces of Ekta's associates Tanushree, Vikas, and some of the other girls—her young team was always invited to her parties—not participating yet, but absorbing the opportunities their new world offered; relishing the idea.

In the centre of the third enclosure, Shobha Kapoor presided over a mammoth table in white make-up, a white sari, and gothic lipstick. She wore rubies and emeralds the size of some exotic animal's eggs. But there was something troublingly familiar about her. An attendant stood patiently behind her holding a crystal bowl of black grapes that she absent-mindedly picked at every few minutes. At one point she stretched out her hand and frowned when she couldn't reach him, and suddenly I knew why she looked so familiar—all the vamps in Ekta's shows, from their clothes down to their intricate bindis—looked remarkably like her mother.

There was no sign yet of Ekta. I was told she liked to make dramatic appearances. Familiar faces from television serials were killing time playing for far lower stakes near the bar. The scalloped ecru curtains had been drawn back, and from across the French windows there was a curious sight. In the adjoining building, standing at the window of their unremarkable two-bedroom flat through which the mussed-up bed and drying towels were visible, Ekta's neighbours were lined up and looking in, stargazing.

At around 2 am a little buzz went around the party. Belying her reputation, Ekta had slipped shyly into the room, dressed in a zardozi lehenga with a pouch dangling from her wrist. For the television crowd, many of whom were there to mark their presence rather than play the great stakes, the party had just gotten underway.

'This is my parents' party, I am just being dutiful here. . . the bashes I throw are more fun, I assure you!'

'But surely this was not going to last long,' I suggested.

'Oh, I don't know, the last time round, because there was no place for me here, I went to my own house and when I returned at eleven the next morning these guys were straggling out.'

She then made her way around the room, stopping at the various tables, asking her friends whether they were winning or losing. When someone made a little pout signalling loss, she took out a fat wad of notes from her batua and gave it to them with a benevolent command, 'Come on, play.' Another wad was similarly offered at another table. Irrespective of losses, the party must continue.

5

Moon Das

'You may not be a celebrity, but you have to behave like one.'

—Moon Das, who was approached to play
Maria Susairaj in a film

OF THE TEN films that were registered on the subject of Neeraj's killing, the quickest off the block was Shakir Shaikh's *Oh! Maria*. Shaikh, fifty-three, is a writer, producer, and director who specializes in making low-budget movies based on sensational real-life events.

His last film, *Mudrank*, was based on the multi-crore stamp paper scam. Abdul Rahim Telgi, the mastermind of India's most audacious financial scandal, was unimpressed by the film's poor production value. 'Had you bothered to meet me earlier, aapki film bade budget ki ho jaati' (Your film would have become a big-budget movie), he told Shaikh the one time they met in jail.

The moderately successful film—in what's called the 'B' circuit—was also endlessly delayed due to legal issues. Yet Shaikh, who continued to favour the all-white uniform popular with Bollywood directors in the eighties, wanted to make another movie on a case that was under trial. He explained why. 'I am not a big moviemaker, and I can never afford to work with stars like Aamir or Shah Rukh Khan. If I make a film on a regular subject, no one will buy it; in such a situation the subject of the film has to be the hero. Logon mein attraction create karna padta hai. . .' *Oh! Maria,* he said, had that potential. He promised the film would be a 'glamour thriller'.

Shakir Shaikh mentioned an actress called Moon Das, whom he wanted to play his leading lady in the role of Maria Susairaj. 'It would be a casting coup,' he was convinced.

Moon Das had already been a tabloid sensation—the showgirl whose spurned boyfriend had killed her mother and uncle, before turning the gun on himself. The third bullet had been intended for Moon, who escaped because she'd been out to dinner with friends.

In the media scrum that followed, Moon, who migrated from Calcutta to Mumbai seeking celebrity, found herself variously portrayed as a harlot, a hard-headed careerist, even a gold-digger. 'Two days after my mother's death a reporter—he was from your newspaper,' she said when we met, 'called to ask me if I had ever been arrested from the Marriott for soliciting. What kind of question is that? Is there no decency?'

These questions followed her wherever she went. No landlord, even in emancipated, seen-it-all Andheri, was willing to rent their home to her. Her old flat at Yamuna Nagar, where the shootout happened, was certified as having 'bad vastu', and so, in this city where a house has greater premium than body and soul, it found no takers. Her younger brother who lived in Calcutta eventually came down to Mumbai and leased a flat for her in his name.

It was a year after the tragic shootout when the neighbours discovered the identity of the young woman living in their midst. Indignation reigned all around, and Moon was asked to vacate the flat. The matter reached the police, and an inspector had to come in to attest to her character before she was allowed to stay on, but only until the lease expired. It would not be renewed.

Shakir Shaikh saw Moon's notoriety merging with his own ambitions—'With her in, the curiosity value would go up even further, it will be easier to sell the film.'

Via via—that great Mumbai modus operandi—he sent her feelers to play the lead role in *Oh! Maria*. Moon, who had been avidly reading about the killing and Maria Susairaj, was not interested. She had set her sights higher. 'I would rather do a small role in a Yash Raj film than play the heroine in some B-grade movie,' she said dismissively. 'This business is all about perception.'

That principle, I was learning, guided her entire life. After giving me the runaround—'I am busy'; 'I am travelling'; 'I am unwell'; 'Talk to my manager' (who did not exist because he had been sacked)—she agreed to meet me. A word from influential quarters, via via, helped.

We met at a coffee shop in Oshiwara. The coffee shop was on the terrace of a building that housed Lebanese,

Chinese and Indian restaurants, hosiery shops, film producers' offices, and most prominently, shared space on the terrace itself with the sprawling Sykz gym, which hosted a constellation of minor stars every evening. There was Koena Mitra, her body evidently touched up by a skilful scalpel; breasts rock steady as she vigorously pounded the treadmill. There was Gauhar Khan crunching her washboard abs under the eagle eye of a personal trainer. Rumour had it that when Ekta Kapoor came in to exercise, even the Jat hunks, usually enraptured by their own pecs in the mirror, swivelled to stare at her.

Coffee guzzlers sat across the glass wall trying to ignore the fishbowl gymnastics. Moon walked in dressed in the fashion of the day, indigo skinny pants, a patterned shirt tucked into them. In her pretty ballerina flats she stood slender and tall. She was striking rather than beautiful, and her startling grey contact lenses gave her a vampiric edge. She ordered a cappuccino, which was discarded after a few sips. The carrot cake was firmly rejected. 'Na baba, I am 58 kilos, I need to be like her,' she said, pointing to Gauhar Khan. 'She is 52 kilos. I need to lose 6 kilos for the music video that I will be doing.'

Both her Hindi and English were mongrelized, and she spoke with a thick Bengali accent that was at odds with her chic appearance. She started the interview as if reading out her résumé. 'I am from central Calcutta. . .' but later, as the formality receded, she became friendlier, more at ease, and corrected herself. 'Actually, I am from North Calcutta, and I studied in a Bengali medium school, which I left half-way through.'

Moon's father owned a furniture workshop in the old market of Bau Bazar, and her mother had been a housewife whose great ambition to dress up like Dimple Kapadia in *Bobby* was thwarted because she married too young, and into a conservative family.

'As a kid I loved watching TV, I was fascinated by models and beauty queens.' She was ten the year Sushmita Sen and Aishwarya Rai were crowned Miss Universe and Miss World, and wanted to wear make-up and strut down the catwalk like the models she admired here. 'Studies didn't interest me one bit. My brother was just the opposite, he's sincere and hard-working when it comes to studies, and which is why he is now in Illinois doing his M.Tech.'

The year she turned seventeen, Shah Rukh Khan came to Calcutta for a show at the Netaji Subhas Bose Indoor Stadium. A friend of Moon's who knew the organizers got her in as one of the models walking on the stage flanking Khan. It was a chance to rub shoulders with the superstar, and the money was good too—Rs 5,000. During the show she befriended two girls, and through them started to get modelling jobs.

'My father was very strict, and totally against my modelling, but since I was sure about what I wanted I began throwing tantrums and stopped eating.' Moon's mother, who had not been allowed to dress like Bobby, became her ally, using silence—that infallible Bramhastra in the battle between men and women. 'She told me that I should go ahead and do all the things she herself couldn't achieve. My mother was just nineteen years older to me; she was my hero, we were best friends,' she said, her eyes welling up. Her grief venting at the slightest impress of memory, she wiped away the tears unselfconsciously and carried on as if interrupted by a sneeze.

Worn down by his daughter's demonstrative rebellion and his wife's silent displeasure, Moon's father relented. She began modelling for catalogues for *Sananda* and the designers Mona Pali. 'I was a good clotheshorse, and soon I started getting noticed. I also had a mixing nature so there were no problems with the other models.' Eventually the family allowed her to travel out of town for shows. 'Since many men in the fashion world were believed to be gay they assumed that I would be safe.'

One day, the owner of the showroom to which her father supplied furniture spotted Moon and approached the family with a proposal of marriage for his son. 'I met this boy under duress, but in the very first meeting I quietly told him to get lost. I had other dreams. I wanted to be this girl from North Calcutta who could go out into the world and do something special. I told my Papa, "I am just eighteen, give me just five–six years, and if in that time I unable to do something special, I will get married to whoever you say."'

In the pre-L'Oreal generation, an academic duffer's best bet was to study home science, and an ad extolling her homely-comely charms in the matrimonial section of a newspaper. But the collective fetishizing of Sushmita Sen, Aishwarya Rai, and Priyanka Chopra as beauty queens opened up a whole world of possibilities for middle class girls who otherwise failed at the Great Indian Crucible: Studies. Now, everyone was worth it, deserving of a stab at the good life. Beauty pageants became the new UPSC. You could be Miss Sector 27, Miss Kanpur, Miss Asia-Pacific, and if all went well, Miss World. Sushmita, Aishwarya, Bipasha, Priyanka—non-graduates all—came to symbolize the resurgent Indian woman. Aware that she would not be able to hold off her father's pressure for long, and desperate for a quick exit from her oppressively conservative environment, Moon entered a beauty pageant.

In the early 1990s Maureen Wadia, the air hostess-turned-socialite wife of the industrialist Nusli Wadia, had the bright idea of launching a magazine and using it as a platform to run a beauty contest, much like *Femina* magazine's Miss India pageant. But unlike *Femina*'s decorous corn-kebab appeal, *Gladrags* was more fun-between-the-sheets, preferably Bombay Dyeing, and for a while the magazine was a big favourite with solo gentlemen travellers on the Rajdhani and Indian Airlines.

The pageant followed in the same vein. It had no inhibitions when it came to blowing its own crumpet. 'My fellow Calcuttan Koena Mitra became famous after participating in the contest. Then John Abraham, whom I just love, had also been a *Gladrags* model. As opposed to the classier *Femina* Miss India, *Gladrags* had a bolder image that suited my outgoing personality better. Besides,' she admitted, 'I also didn't have the educational qualification for *Femina* Miss India, as I had not cleared high school.'

She was shortlisted from the east zone, and called to Mumbai. It was to be her first exposure to the competitive megawatt world of Mumbai models. 'They were bitchy and made fun of me that I could not speak properly, meaning I lacked English [skills].' Undeterred by the jibes, Moon chose to speak in Hindi on stage, which led the actor Anil Kapoor to cheer for her. Among the judges, unbelievably, was John Abraham. She stayed on in Mumbai for twenty one days. 'It was fantastic, I could go anywhere, at any time, do what I liked. I realized that in this city everything depends on you. Nothing else matters, and that was such a heady discovery. "'Yehi ek jagah hai," I told myself, "where I can have a free life."'

When her horrified father refused to let her move to Mumbai, Moon went on a hunger strike, and then took it further by swallowing a handful of sleeping pills—'Just enough to knock me out but not kill me.' Once again, Moon's father was forced to back down, and matters proceeded swiftly. She contacted a real estate broker who had advertised in the classified section of the tabloid that had carried her photograph from the contest. On July 12, 2004, Moon Das, aged twenty, landed at her Rs 5,500 a month PG at RNA Arcade, Andheri.

Her first move was to call up the models she met during the *Gladrags* contest, who had promised her work. 'I would spend hours at the nearby STD booth every day trying to call them and other people who might help, but no one had any time for me. I was so bewildered, this wasn't the Bombay I had imagined, and I didn't know how to break through this wall.' There was no one to entertain her tears, or to yield to her tantrums. 'After a month of this my landlady advised me to go back home and I thought it would indeed be the best course.'

But then the via via line crackled to life. 'Kapil Khanna, a 2002 *Gladrags* model whom I had managed to get in touch with through some people, phoned me, inviting me to a Page 3 party.' Moon could not recall who the host was or even where the party was, but distinctly remembered what she wore: a white corset teamed with a yellow micro-mini. 'That's because I got so many compliments, everyone looked at me that evening and someone even clicked my picture.'

As with the very young, it took just one evening of fun to erase the misery of the month, and Moon resolved to stay put. Her friendship with Kapil Khanna deepened, and he helped her negotiate through the maze of advertising agencies and model coordinators.

'I began the rounds of auditions and soon I was doing print ads for Kelvinator, Durian, Roopam. . . I shifted to a PG in Bandra, taking buses everywhere to save money. During this period my mother and I spoke a hundred times a day, I shared every minute thing that happened through the day. Reliance had just introduced the Rs 1 per minute talktime scheme; my mother and I made full use of that. For the last four years I've been their platinum customer. Gradually, I also started doing shows, travelling to Goa, Pune, Nagpur, Ahmedabad, gaining in confidence with each show. Now, if someone made fun of my lack of English, or my accent, I'd smartly turn around and say, 'Aap Bangla mein bol ke dikhao.' (Why don't you speak in Bengali?)

The attitude was in place, but she lacked the sophistication and skill to become a top-rung model. Intense competition and poor diction also ruled out films and television, leaving ambitious Moon with the option of becoming that uniquely Bollywood creation, an 'item girl'.

But even that breakthrough would not be easy—there were A-list heroines competing for item songs in the big films. With movies still out of her reach and bump-n-grind girls Rakhi Sawant and Meghna Naidu well entrenched in the music video scene, Moon, ready to pay her dues, set her sights lower. This was the time when the world was outsourcing to India, and 'Bangalored' became an acceptable verb. The sensex was pole-vaulting above 20,000, and corporate India was full of Big Boys Who Played at Night.

'Almost every second or third week one company or the other would have its annual conference, off-site meetings, or dinners for dealers. The standard entertainment here would be a live show. Typically, a troupe comprised a singer, say Abhijit, Juggy D, or one of the contestants from music talent shows like *Sa Re Ga Ma*. In addition, there would be a mimicry artist, usually from *Laughter Challenge*, and the grand finale would be a performance by an item girl.' After which the sexed-up but too-sozzled-to-do-anything men would head home feeling vaguely satiated. This suited Moon who told me, without any sense of irony, that she had become famous in the dealer circuit as a 'hot performer'.

Since then the economic downturn had been unkind. Corporate perquisites vanished, leaving Moon and others like her to slip even further down the ladder. When we met, she had just returned from Bilaspur, where she was performing at a Sikh wedding. 'It was so dull, I tell you. These people were a blight on the name of their usually lively community. We had to literally plead with them to clap. Poor Vinit [one of the winners of a television talent hunt, and now a playback singer] sang for six hours and I made four entries.' The number of entries is important, she stressed. A dancer must not do too many encores, as it brings down her value, and at each entry a group of at least six background dancers must first get on stage before the main item girl makes an appearance.

'When you are wearing itsy-bitsy clothing and gyrating to provocative songs, dancing solo on stage makes you look cheap, whereas with some girls in the background the same thing looks like an item song, just like in the movies. You may not be a celebrity,' she told me, 'but you have to behave like one.'

'Do you know how expensive it is to look like one? One good lipstick costs a thousand rupees, then there is perfume, expensive shades—that's very, very important if you have to pass off as a star, good shoes are a must, you should carry Samsonite luggage, an expensive handbag like the Esbeda Swarovski bag or something similar. Also I make sure that I never pick up my bags, and even though I am happy drinking tap water, I'll always insist on mineral water. Sometimes on these long shows, I get really hungry but I will not sit with everyone and eat. I'd rather go hungry. This business is all about projection.'

Typically, this was the list of conditions that was sent to the organizer before a show:

1. The artist will charge Rs X (the fee can vary from Rs 35,000 to Rs 70,000 per show).
2. Fifty percent of the agreed amount will be paid upfront and the rest after the show.
3. The artist will not make more than four entries.
4. The windows of the artist's green room should be covered with thick dark curtains or black paper ('to keep out the peeping toms').
5. There will be at least six background dancers.
6. Return air ticket, but not on budget airlines, only Jet or Kingfisher.
7. The vehicle at the airport should be worth at least Rs ten lakh. ('That's just to say I don't want to get out of the airport and get into a Maruti 800, you know.')
8. Five-star accommodation ('if it's a small town like Ranchi, Bilaspur, a three-star hotel').
9. Hotel stay to be fully paid for by the organizer.
10. Transport available at all times.
11. Two security guards to accompany the artist.

Moon would not do private shows—the kind wealthy businessmen organized at farmhouses—those were best left to out-of-work bar girls. Moon explained that she was popular at weddings because she was always good to the women of the house. 'People notice me, I know how to carry myself. I have a sparkle and that becomes dangerous for me [vis-à-vis the men], so I always make it a point to put the women at ease. For instance, if we are posing for a picture I'll always get the women of the family in the centre saying it's their day and not mine. This floors them, and I get a good reputation.

'We may have become jaded about celebrities in the big cities, but the small towns are where the action is. They still have to experience a lot of the world and wahan logon ke paas kuan bhar paisa hai [People in small towns have a hoard of wealth]. I recently travelled to Kishangarh where the host has a haveli worth Rs 35 crore.' And she was recently back from performing at a Shivratri mela at Pratapgarh, which is flush with NRI funds. But this dancing at shaadi, mela, mundan was becoming a bit tiresome.

'I wish I could do some serious arty film, you know play a Naxalwadi.'

'Why specifically a Naxalite?' I asked.

'Why not? I am Bengali and with a shaari and dark make-up I could pass for a decent Naxalwadi.'

She did get a few offers to feature in music videos. 'I was asked to be one of the models dancing with Abhishek Bachchan in '*Dus bahane kar ke le gaye dil*'; there was another offer to be one of the sidekicks in a Deepal Shaw video. I turned them all down. There is no point in being one of the anonymous faces behind these guys. Likewise, I don't want to work in any Punjabi or Bhojpuri film. I am very careful about my family's izzat. I would never want my dad to go to the market and there see a poster of some sleazy Adults-only Bhojpuri film with my face and cleavage plastered on it.'

As I got to know Moon better, I realized that despite the grind that show business demands of ambitious women, there was something of the vestal virgin about her. So she would wear minuscule clothing, slap on cosmetics that made her look older, and dance with heavy thrusting movements, but all of it was pantomime. Away from the stage, her quotidian relationship with men was friendly but determinedly asexual.

When her manager tried to get into her bed, she sacked him. 'We were in Aurangabad for a show and he told me that he would be sharing the room with me. I told him, "Saada," she lisped, "you are my manager, don't cross your limit," and I sacked him.'

During one of our meetings, she used the phrase 'sex symbol' to describe herself. When I asked her to explain, she paused. 'On the New Year's Eve of 2006 I was invited for a show at Hotel Mayfair in Rourkela. When I reached there I saw my pictures had been plastered all over town, announcing my show. There was a mini-riot for passes in Rourkela that day. I was told paanch logon ka sar phoot gaya [five people had their heads smashed in]. It wouldn't be so for a plain girl, would it?'

At this show, Moon was introduced to Avinash Patnaik. He was a friend of the organizer. 'The show was a big hit. I wore my item girl clothes and danced to songs like '*Kajra re*', '*Saaki saaki re*'. . . In all I did four entries, and the entire performance lasted twenty-five minutes.' After the resounding whistles, she returned to her room for a solitary TV dinner when the organizer came knocking. He was accompanied by Avinash, and they said they would like to show her around Rourkela. 'They drove me around and took me for coffee to the local college canteen. It was a nice friendly interaction. I thought to myself, "They are village boys and I should be good to them." I barely noticed Avinash as he hardly spoke, but when they dropped me back to my room, I told them, half in jest, "If you come to Mumbai, get in touch with me, and I too will show you around my city." I think for Avinash it was a big deal that a woman like me was talking to him.'

Emboldened, he began to call her frequently once she returned to Mumbai. 'I was always polite, friendly.' One day, not long after her show, he landed in Mumbai. 'He said he was going to take me up on my offer to show him around. Then the next day he asked me if I could help get him a makeover. Now, I have a big thing for clothes and when I am with people I always want them to dress up well. He was not very good-looking; he used to wear tight jeans and shoes with elevator heels so I thought I could help him. Over two days, I took him shopping, got his hair coloured, facial done, and also took him to a party at Rock Bottom.'

Was that just philanthropic instinct, or something more, I asked.

'I had been in Mumbai for two years, managing everything on my own. I had a busy life, but I was also quite lonely. I wanted to settle down but I was clear that it could not be with anyone from the entertainment industry or the corporate sector. I had seen how promiscuous they are. Do drink ke baad they have no idea, tie kahaan aur shirt kahaan.'

'Avinash was persistent, he seemed sweet. He had a rice mill, was well settled, and I thought he would respect me because for him I was a big cheez.'

Moon could not have been more wrong.

The boy from Rourkela wooed the sex symbol from Mumbai with grand gestures. On Valentine's Day, he deposited Rs five lakh in her account, saying she should use the money to make a music video. It was only later she found out that the money was not his to give away. They swiftly fell into a relationship. When they met, it was with the intensity of long-distance lovers. 'Avinash was my first boyfriend. Before that, when I was about sixteen, I had been infatuated with a Punjabi boy back home in Calcutta—he looked like Sunny Deol, he was well built and six foot two but he strung me along and nothing ever came of it, I was very hurt by that.'

But as the first flush of the new relationship faded, Moon realized her boyfriend was not the wealthy man he had made himself out to be. His father had taken a Rs two crore loan to set up a rice mill for him, which Avinash was squandering away. 'When I realized that he was under tremendous financial pressure I decided to spend the money he had given me back on him.' Moon was desperate to clear the charge that she used Avinash for money, showing me signed blank cheques he had given her and which she never deposited.

Like Emile Jerome had with Maria, Avinash began to get cloyingly possessive, wanting to know where she was going, who she was meeting, and to what end. He would often fly into a jealous rage. To avoid that, she would call him before going in for meetings and keep her phone on throughout, so he could listen in on what was going on.

'Basically,' she said with a moue, 'he started showing boyfriendgiri.' The relationship, barely a few months old, disintegrated rapidly even though she insisted she was in love with him. 'He was insanely jealous.' They would have the most corrosive fights on the phone. 'What do you want with my body?' I'd ask him. 'Kaat kaat ke namak bharoge kya?' Ultimately I told him that these fights were not acceptable, and if he had such a problem with my work, he should set up a boutique for me in Orissa and we should get married.'

Avinash was introduced to her parents; her father took an instant dislike to him but once again, against her father's wishes, Moon followed him to Rourkela. 'One evening he told me to wear skimpy clothes and go with him to a discotheque.' He was hoping to get a loan from the owner of the discotheque and Moon was to be future collateral. 'I was aghast that this man who wanted to marry me wanted to display me in such a manner, and we had a fight right there.'

That night was the first time Avinash slapped Moon. 'Thwack! It was a full-blooded slap right across my face. All my life I'd been a girl without fear, but that moment changed it forever.' Desperately afraid, but with no way of leaving Rourkela at that hour she went back to Avinash's home where he did something she understood all too well: he took a handful of sleeping pills. She waited out the night, knowing it wouldn't kill him. The next morning brought remorse, recrimination, and decision. Avinash took Moon to a temple and there the two exchanged garlands and got married, Hindi film style. The more she regretted her relationship, the more impelled she felt to submit to his wishes. He told her to return to Mumbai and promised to come and get her as soon as his finances improved.

'But within four days of my getting back to Mumbai he landed at my house, which I was then sharing with my maternal uncle, who knew nothing of my relationship with Avinash, it was all quite awkward.'

On his second day in Mumbai, Avinash borrowed Rs 4,000 from Moon to buy cocaine. All vestiges of the loving, reverential man were gone. 'When I returned home from a meeting he was like a crazed animal, sniffing me up and down; he thought I had gone out and slept with someone else.'

'The day after that we went to a mall, where we had another argument and he pulled my hair and hit me so hard my lip split open and my face went numb.' She fished out her cellphone and showed me a picture that she took of herself: her face was bruised and tumescent, like a piece of rotten fruit. 'When my uncle saw me he threw a fit—he called my mother and asked her to come over from Calcutta immediately, after which he and I together forced Avinash to leave.' Over the next several days, Avinash called, pleaded, wept, threatened, cajoled, raved, ranted, and then fell ominously silent.

Happy to have her mother in Mumbai, and free of the bitter fights with Avinash, Moon immersed herself in work and friends. On November 22, 2007, as she was driving to the airport for a meeting with LG Electronics, her friend got a call on his cell. It was Avinash, saying he had landed in Mumbai. Determined to keep misgivings at bay, Moon went on to her meeting and after that for dinner at the Garden Court restaurant in Andheri. 'I rang my mother, as I always did every few hours. The phone kept ringing but no one picked up. I called my mama, his phone too went unanswered. I kept trying but there were just long rings and no answer. The food turned to ashes in my mouth. My friend Ramesh and I rushed home.'

When she reached her home at Parasrampuria Towers, she saw the watchman ambling in the compound, children playing, and Avinash's black Honda City snaked between the parked cars, its windows hooded. Like Emile's sudden journey from Kochi to Mumbai, Avinash had driven all the way from Orissa, but the 1,200 kilometre journey had done nothing to extinguish his rage. 'The car was locked, he wasn't in. We raced up the stairs and rang the bell. After a few seconds the door opened partially—it never opened fully because there was a shoe rack kept behind it—and Avinash looked out. I could see no one behind him. He stared at me, then at Ramesh, and then just as I made to enter he grabbed my hand and tried to yank me in.' That gesture and the fact that the door did not open fully probably saved her life. 'I screamed and Ramesh pulled me back. We slammed the door shut, and latching it from outside, ran all the way to the Oshiwara police station.

Moon came back accompanied by the police to find blood all over her tiny flat. Avinash lay in the living room, the blood seeping out of his forehead where he had shot himself with the gun—a desi revolver—still warm next to him. On the kitchen floor lay the colder bodies of her uncle and beloved mother. She has tried to imagine what could have transpired in that one-bedroom flat a million times since. Did he kill them right away; did he torture and kill them; were they alive when she had first reached home?

For now there is immense anger in her over what followed. Like Neeraj Grover's and Emile Jerome's fathers did with Maria, Avinash's father blamed Moon for his son's downfall; he called her a good-time girl on the make and accused her of siphoning off funds from his son. 'Avinash was a weak man, he was a coward with grand ambitions. He wanted to become an Ambani overnight, but was not willing to work for it. He was a failure and he took out his frustrations on me. But the media reserved all its sympathy for him, he was treated like some jilted lover. But don't you see, I am the one who lost everything that day.'

'I, not my mother, not my mama, should have died that day. . . I have so much guilt. After the funeral I haven't had the courage to see my father. My father, who was so opposed to my coming to Mumbai, asked me only one thing, "Did you do anything wrong?" When I said no, he told me, "You must stay on in Mumbai and fulfil all your mother's dreams." When I first came here this city represented freedom but now to establish myself here has become a goal.'

She crammed her days with work: Morning 10 am–12 pm was reserved for Bollywood dance class, 2–4 pm was spent gymming at Sykz, 5.30–8 pm was for the acting class. 'I have now become really serious about work, I will do whatever it takes to improve myself and live down this scandalous image. Once I have cleared my name I will go back to Calcutta, adopt a child, and live with my father. I am no longer interested in men.'

Unfortunately for Moon, the reverse was not true. One day while indulging in that other vanity, Googling herself, Moon discovered a website dedicated to her: www.moondas.com. The site was maintained by a man she had briefly befriended during her search for a manager. 'But this man tried to act oversmart, so I dropped him.' Now she discovered pictures of herself and a couple of fanzine-style articles that labelled her a call girl on this site. Unsurprisingly, there was a roster of comments that sickened her. She filed a complaint with the Cyber Crime Investigation Cell of the Mumbai police, asking for the site to be blocked and action taken against the site's manager. The cops did little, telling her they could not locate him, which was a joke because just a few days later she found the man (who had previously been booked for defrauding women through a dating site) sitting in a cyber café.

'I ran to the Oshiwara police station where they know me well, got two cops who arrested him and handed him to the cyber cell. But there,' she paused, looking incredulous, 'they let him go. Report at eleven o'clock the next morning, they told him.' Dutifully she also went to the cyber cell office located in the Fort area of south Mumbai, the other end of the city for Moon. 'I kept waiting but just as I had feared, the manager did not turn up. I was so tired, so angry, so frustrated.' When she complained to a policeman she was told insolently, 'If you're getting so harassed, why don't you go and catch him for us.'

'I just snapped, I turned around and told him, "Sir, that's exactly what I did but you let him go." So this man, Parmar or something, looks me up and down and says, "No point in waiting here. Why don't you go and watch some film. There is *Drona* and *Kidnap* playing. Watch a movie for a few hours and come back, then we'll see what we can do."

'I felt so helpless, so humiliated, I came out of there and started crying.'

She contacted a friend in the media, who suggested that she go and complain to Rakesh Maria, then chief of the Crime Branch, since she was in the vicinity of his office. 'Maria sir heard me out, then he picked up the phone and in front of me he lambasted those guys and instructed his people to arrest the manager.'

A few days after my meeting with Moon, I met Rakesh Maria at his office to discuss Neeraj's killing. I was hoping to get more details about the investigation and the prosecution's case. It was a Saturday, and despite the frequent phone calls and chits from visitors, he was relaxed and inclined to talk. We discussed the case, Neeraj's father, the psychology of criminals, and the changing value system.

'The small-town kids coming in to the big cities have no cocooning effect of the family. The old system where families collectively took decisions has given way to children making all the calls. Kids are like gladiators, left to perform, and so they do anything to succeed,' said Rakesh Maria. 'I see so many girls coming from outside to make it big in the film industry. Typically they get in touch with the light men, cameramen, make-up artists, PRs, and on their assurance they just land in Mumbai without any support system and get into all kinds of traps. Just the other day this girl—' he struggled for a few seconds—'the one whose boyfriend killed her mother. . . Moon Das, she came to me with some similar problem. . .'

I saw Moon again that evening. I had come to enjoy our meetings. She was sharp and disarmingly candid, letting me into her world with a touching level of trust. She was all smiles, and the small victory with the cops gave her faith. 'I feel I am getting stronger, I am in a position to protest. Now I need to get my base right, and things will be fine. I am so grateful to Maria sir, he is such a gentleman.'

As part of her resolve to create a new life for herself, Moon decided to assume a new identity, a new name. She had decided to call herself Anushkaa Daas, to lose weight, and to focus on featuring in a music video. 'You must understand the importance of music videos. Rakhi [Sawant] did one, 'Pardesia', and look where she is now, likewise Meghna Naidu did 'Kaliyon ka Chaman' and she became famous overnight. I need something like that.' However, she conceded in the same breath that her timing might have been slightly off. 'The novelty of the raunchy music video has worn off. Now you have to pay the music company before they'll do a video with you rather than the other way round. But you know, my numerologist has told me that with my new name things are bound to change. Moon ka number 4 is not compatible with my destiny number.'

Just as Soho has its sex shops, Charminar its bangles, Castro its gay community, and Ginza its boutiques, Oshiwara has its clairvoyants, astrologers, vastu consultants, gemologists, tarot card readers, rune readers, aura diviners, and numerologists. A favourable horoscope will have greater equity at Ekta Kapoor's Balaji than mere talent, Karan Johar will not make any moves without first consulting his confidante-cum-tarot reader Sunita Menon, the actress Kirron Kher will only travel on certain seat numbers of an aircraft, and Rakesh Roshan, his talented son notwithstanding, will only title his film with the letter K.

'A tarot reader and a personal numerologist are the industry's new status symbols,' Rajorshe P. Das told me when we met at Indigo, Andheri's hip new café, whose design and cuisine aspire to New York standards. When I asked for directions, I was told it was located bang opposite the office of a famous palmist.

Das was the man behind Moon's name change, the one who told her to never wear a diamond, for it would be like zeher (poison) for her. 'There's a sparkle inside her and the added sparkle of the diamond will make men behave aggressively towards her.'

Das looked like he had not bathed in days, and there was a shifty-eyed smarminess to his manner that raised my hackles. People born under the numbers 8, 17, 26, 4, 13, 22, 31, 2, and 20 were bound for a troublesome life, he said, scratching his unshaven cheek, while those with numbers 10, 20, 30 were very unlucky. 'That hardly leaves anyone happy, does it?' I couldn't help but laugh openly. 'The future of Mumbai is not good, he continued calmly. 'I foresee bloodshed and regionalism. Bombay was a better name, the numbers 4, 6, 4, 2, 1, 1 that represent Mumbai are not auspicious.'

'In that case, why did you bother to come here from Calcutta?' I asked, now flaunting my scepticism. Rajorshe P. Das, desperately hoping to distract his hostile interviewer, asked for my birth date to predict my future—I curtly refused, bringing the doomed interview to a close.

Diwali fell a few days later, and I got this text message from him: 'Let this deepawali be a connotation between u and n positiue energies. U will never surrendes to any evil forcfs. – Rajorshe p das'. I spent a few happy minutes contemplating the future of a person whose business depended on spelling-based predictions.

I also made the reporter's cardinal error of being blinkered by my own biases. Less than a month after my meeting with Rajorshe, ten men wafted into Mumbai in a dinghy, holding it hostage for three days. I recalled his prediction about bloodshed in the city. So we met again, this time on his turf and on his terms. Ever the unctuous salesman, he glossed over our previous unpleasant interaction and readily opened up about his life.

Rajorshe Das had enrolled to study science at Dibrugarh University in Assam, but quit before he could complete his degree, instead joining the Indian Air Force as ground staff in the accounts and logistics department of the airbase. It was a monotonous life, he said. 'You know the type where each time, unfailingly, two plus two would be four, and never another variant.' He took an early discharge and moved to Calcutta to learn occult sciences from a guru. He also started making predictions. 'By reading books you can become a wise person but to be able to predict you need to be a spiritual body.'

'In those days I didn't charge money but found that if you offer something for free, people don't value it.' Still unhappy with his stagnant life, Rajorshe decided to take drastic action and add a 'P' to his name—becoming Rajorshe P. Das—and he changed his signature from Bangla to English.

With a flourish, he took my notebook and demonstrated the two signatures. 'Can you see the one in Bangla is all scattered whereas in English it's compact, focused? As I changed my sign, my energies too started getting focused.' His long-pending divorce came through ('If I go for marriage now it'll only be with a woman whose number is 2 or 7.' What's more important, I asked, the right woman or the right number? He did not hesitate: 'The right number').

He was also told by his guru that if he lived by the sea somewhere in the west his life would change. So Rajorshe P. Das came to live by the sea, in an ocean of anxious, insecure, ambitious, competitive, vulnerable, and often rudderless people. He set himself up as a numerologist, charging Rs 2,500 for three sessions, and a thousand extra for house visits. As predicted by his guru, business flourished; from changing names, dictating licence plates, and cell numbers to changing addresses, his writ runs large.

'Now you can get homes that are numerologically compatible.' He did not have an office ('According to my prediction, I shouldn't have an office'), and instead operated from the cafés and coffee shops that dotted Andheri. He met clients at Rivedo café, the Barista at Versova, and Shreeji restaurant right below Nirvana, where Maria's friend Deepak Singh held auditions. Usually the clients footed the bill, but in case they didn't it was just the coffee he had to pay for.

'All my clients are twenty-five and below. Hundred percent of them have bad emotional lives, I have not yet met a single client who is in a stable relationship.' He called this the peril of a 'polygamous life'.

'You see these kids, they look so smart, they wear branded clothes and they walk and talk as if they will conquer the world in a chutki. But when they come to me, all it takes is ten seconds for them to crumble.' With the exception of one or two, his clientele consisted almost entirely of people who had come from outside Mumbai. 'These small town men and women, they make the money but they have no emotional back-up.'

'Everything is different here. The men come to me for relationship advice and the women for better lifestyle and finances.' He said he wanted to learn Kabbalah next, since that was 'the new status symbol'. Aside from clients who come to him through word of mouth, house parties were Rajorshe's happy hunting ground. 'It's very important to network, to know people and through some reference to get invited to house parties where you meet even more people.' He said he never introduced himself to people as a numerologist; instead he got someone else to introduce him that way. 'That has more effect. Then once I get their date of birth I take over because I am good at what I do.' But there was a flip side to networking at parties, he said: 'You can't have fun. You have to be constantly alert for a possible client, hold your drinks, and make an impression. . . There is so much music and sex in the air, woh sab ko dabaa ke [to suppress all that], to be conscious is a punishment.'

As much of a counsellor as a numerologist, he was gung-ho about his future in Mumbai. 'If I continue with this I can shine like anything.' But at the moment he was unhappy with Moon aka Anushkaa. 'Just see the difference... Mooooon,' he made a low sound, 'it sounds so weak. Then say Anush-kaa,' he continued, throwing his voice. 'Isn't that full of impact? But she hasn't been following my advice.'

But Moon, who knew the perils of anonymity and the importance of perception, swiftly understood the value of her name. Much as she may want to escape her notoriety, the name Moon Das had also given her recognition, a toe-hold in the glamour world. The name evoked vague recollection, curiosity, and at least got her past the security guards at studios. As Anushkaa she was just another face, another lithe body running on the treadmill at Sykz, clocking the kilometres but getting nowhere.

With the prospect of a music video seeming increasingly remote, Moon had a new ambition—to participate in a reality TV show like *Bigg Boss*. If Monica Bedi, starlet-turned-moll to the gangster Abu Salem, could get on that show, why couldn't she? Even Maria Susairaj was likely to be offered a slot on the show after her release. 'Mere saath to crime hua hai. If I can get on the show the world will be able to see the real me. I just want them to know that I am not a cheap girl.'

Post the saas–bahu sarson-da-sagas, Indian television was awash with tacky reality TV programmes, formats imported from the West. Most of these shows hosted an assortment of P.T. Barnum-style circus freaks, and encourage bickering, bitching, and bad-mouthing. Moon, with what she called her 'back story', thought she was a perfect fit for some of these shows. But before that, there were other challenges to be dealt with.

The first anniversary of her mother's death was approaching, and she couldn't summon the nerve to return to Calcutta to face her father and neighbours. She fell ill with severe gastroenteritis, brought on by poor eating and stress, and had to get herself admitted to a nursing home in the middle of the night. She told me all this on the phone one day, sounding rather depressed. I invited her for lunch to Oh! Calcutta, hoping it would cheer her up. We ordered cold beer, aloo dum, bhetki, and loochi. She was clearly tempted—'I really miss Bengali food'—but she wouldn't touch more than a few morsels, as always, leaving food on her plate. She discussed her anxiety about meeting her father. 'I respect him a lot but don't share much with him, it was different with my mother. But then, who else is there to guide me? Sometimes it's so tiring, I have to take all the decisions by myself.'

We sat in companionable silence until she spoke up again in a low voice: 'Mujhe Ishu ke sharan mein aana hai' (I want to be under Jesus' shelter). I did a quick alcohol check, but we were still on our first pint. Her friends, the actress Vaishnavi and the singer Jimmy Felix, had been reading to her from the Bible and demonstrating His miracles.

'Vaishnavi showed me the dengue report of a girl which was positive in the morning but after prayers turned negative. Likewise Rakhi Sawant's mother had gallstones which disappeared overnight after prayers. My father has been diagnosed with high blood pressure and gastroenteritis, I worry for him, and generally I want peace. I am told confession is good for the soul. The pastors told me that maybe my mother and mama have not forgiven me for causing their deaths, so I need to seek forgiveness. My entire family is suffering. Pastors told me that often there is doubt followed by fear but all that is mitigated if you leave everything to Jesus.'

She then called Vaishnavi and arranged to meet her in the evening at the church. A few days later I got a call from Moon, who said that she had been shortlisted by Synergie Adlabs, where Neeraj last worked, to participate in *Sach ka Saamna,* modelled on the format of *Moment of Truth,* where contestants were put through a polygraph test. They got paid for accurately answering a set of questions and there was a jackpot at the end. But as the stakes went up the questions got more personal, more intrusive. 'I am not afraid of these questions, it'll give me a chance to clear my name. I think it's a miracle of God that I got this call. Once I get a clean chit and people know that I didn't use Avinash, that I am a good girl, I can go back to live in Calcutta.'

I did not hear from Moon for some time after that meeting. Three months later I saw billboards all over Mumbai announcing a new dance competition on television called *Dancing Queen,* with Moon striking a pose in the line-up of contestants. I called to congratulate her and she invited me to her new apartment. She opened the door dressed in a buttoned-up nightie and Daffy Duck slippers. Her hair was in a ponytail and she looked well scrubbed, healthy, and happy. 'This flat has positive vibrations and is considered a lucky house in Shastri Nagar. All the previous residents like Gracy Singh, Rahul Roy, Vaishnavi, Deepak Tijori have gone on to buy their own apartments.'

As we caught up she told me that she did go to Calcutta for the anniversary of her mother's death, and stayed on for eighteen days. 'I looked after my father, got his check-ups done, bought him new clothes, organized the house, and helped my brother shop before he left for Illinois.'

'My father,' she looked up, 'he behaved very well with me. There was a guy who has been wanting to marry me, despite everything that has happened. But my father told him now is not the time, that I was doing things with my life. Imagine! He said that. Which is why, though the prize money was Rs one crore I decided against doing *Sach ka Saamna*. They ask all kinds of questions. It's okay to answer questions on Avinash, but there would also be questions like how often I have sex, how many boyfriends I have had. I can't answer those in front of my father.'

Dancing Queen approached her because 'everybody on that show had a story, and they liked mine'. Other participants included a former dance bar girl who had fallen on bad times, a girl who was dancing to save her AIDS-stricken friend, and yet another participant with leucoderma, fighting to gain acceptance in society.

Though she was knocked out of the competition halfway through, she performed to the chartbuster of the time, A.R. Rahman's 'Masakkali,' in a special episode. It's a song about setting a caged bird free. 'It couldn't be closer to my life. *Dancing Queen* has really set me free.'

'Ever since Jesus has come into my life, my life has changed. My equation with my father improved, I've started getting good work, my brother got his visa to the United States, I got this house. . .'

The house had a sofa, a couple of mattresses piled up on the floor, a television and a stereo system covered by a sheet, and a teetering rack of CDs. On one of the walls was a large framed poster of Moon in her oomphy avatar, lips curled in an exaggerated pout; and in the same room there was a picture of her without make-up posing with her brother. Finally, the two Moons coexisting in the same space without conflict.

As she watched me looking around the room, she said, 'All my earlier houses were just places to shack up because I always believed that I was here in Mumbai for a short while and then I'd go back to Calcutta. But see how I have done up this house—Mumbai is home now, and if that is to be so I must live in it properly.'

6

Ram Gopal Varma

'Power and sex are the only two realities of life.'

—Ram Gopal Varma, director of *Not a Love Story*, inspired by the Neeraj Grover case

Ram Gopal Varma's office is at the edge of Oshiwara, where the middle class ghetto of Millat Nagar tapers into the swamp. It's distinguished by the director's personal vehicle, a Land Rover that is nearly as wide as the street, and his slew of young male assistants.

Inside the office, bereft of any feminine presence, Ramu, as he is known in Bollywood, sits in a chilled, windowless, vault-like room. Thick glazed paper, patterned with globes and assorted world maps, covers the walls. From behind a formidable desk, the master of this universe was waging a battle for the many virtues of Maria Susairaj.

In appearance he may be closer to Sancho Panza, but Ramu is Bollywood's Don Quixote, tilting at the windmills. Appalled by the media vilification following the court verdict, he tweeted endlessly in defence of Maria, taking on irate anchors, even mischievously offering to cast her in a film.

This is the kind of impishness that made him rename one of his biggest duds *Ram Gopal Varma Ki Aag*, and get into a Twitter war with the director Karan Johar who said the promos of *Phoonk 2* were so 'scary' that he'd have to see the film with the director—to which Ramu snidely responded saying he was fine as long as Karan did not insist on holding his hand.

While he was at school in Hyderabad, he was often bullied, he told me. Now that he is all grown up (though his one-time collaborator Mani Ratnam insists he still isn't), Ramu has developed the appetite for a good scrap, and a near-obsession with the psychology of violence. His last happy film—not necessarily for the distributors—was the delightful caper *Daud* in 1997.

While others hemmed and hawed and cast and canned, the prolific director, who often churns out up to three films a year, finished *Not a Love Story*, 'inspired' by Neeraj's death, in five months flat. His budget: Rs three crore, the same amount Ekta had planned to spend on her Neeraj Grover film. Emile Jerome's lawyer, Wahab Khan, who Ramu interviewed for his research, could not believe the film had been finished so quickly. 'But he just met me two months ago!'

On the other hand, Maria's lawyer Sharif Shaikh, who refused to cooperate on the film, said he was contemplating legal action against it and asked Ramu to show him the film before release.

On the morning of the court verdict, there were full page advertisements for the movie in the newspapers, and by afternoon, as judge M.W. Chandwani read out from his 175-page-long judgment, Ramu had released a trailer. It was an arresting teaser, featuring a man and a woman swabbing blood from an apartment floor before going on to make love, while an inert foot jutted into the frame. The catch line read: 'In the summer of 2008. . .two lovers did a terrible thing. . .'

The use of the word 'terrible' is clever. It's not meant to condemn—rather to titillate, rousing the voyeur in his audience. The idea of two people making love next to a dead man had caught his imagination, and became the point from where Ramu spun the love story. 'The title is deliberately misleading,' he said, with a happy grin. Once again, Maria's confession became instrumental in perpetuating the urban legend of Neeraj's death.

In a clever riff on one of his most loved films, Ramu recorded a slower version of the title song from *Rangeela* and used it on Mahie Gill, the actress who played Maria, as she swirled across the screen in a gown that appeared ominously red. 'I see Maria as the girl who wanted to be famous. Had she succeeded, she would have become a celebrity actress like Milee, Urmila's character in *Rangeela,* but she didn't, instead ending up infamous as a murder accomplice. It's just a matter of circumstance.'

He is so caught up with the drama of Maria's life and the 'dignity with which she conducted herself' at the press conference called by her lawyer, that he laughingly confessed to being 'half in love with her'.

There are some themes that recur with monotonous frequency in his films: the moral void, the claustrophobic apartment setting, and memorably, the swaying derrière of his leading ladies. *Not a Love Story* has all these motifs.

He seemed pleased at the mention. 'Power and sex are the only two realities of life.'

Ram Gopal Varma on a roll is one of journalism's guilty pleasures. He is a terrific raconteur, offering sharp (if often deliberately provocative) insights, and is utterly droll, delivering one wisecrack after another, managing to look poker-faced and wild-eyed at the same time.

A typical RGV-ism is: 'Shah Rukh Khan is confidence personified, because he is very bright. Salman Khan is confidence personified because he is very dumb.'

He also understands the delusions of stardom—the non-stop hustling, and above all the overarching ambition that crackles through the lanes he inhabits. 'There's this woman, an aspiring actress, who sends me risqué jokes and messages every night. After a certain hour of the night, if a woman you don't know sends you such sexy jokes, it means something. But if your desire to become an actress is greater than anything else, then offering a sexual favour is a very small price [to pay], and you will not mind it.'

He never responds to her, has never met her, having rejected her photographs, but her persistence keeps up their non-relationship; a bunny-boiler's obsession that he will no doubt mime cinematically some day. Like Ekta's stalker who infiltrated the Balaji office disguised as a pandit, there was a young man who stood outside his home for over a year and a half. 'No matter what time of the day I emerged, he would be there—all he wanted to do was greet me; it was spooky.'

After he created such unlikely stars as Manoj Bajpai and Rajpal Yadav, and acquired a reputation as Bollywood's talent spotter—Anurag Kashyap, Shimit Amin, and Jaideep Sahni all began their careers with Ramu—aspirants started thronging his office night and day. 'There are people, literally unwashed masses, who come to his office directly from Mumbai Central station. They'll come with a suitcase and two crumpled pages of a storyline, pleading for an audience with Ramuji for just two minutes,' a former colleague said.

That is about all the time he has to spare. Famously, he doesn't conduct auditions. In the time it takes for an aspiring actor to walk from the reception and open the glass door to his office, Ramu makes up his mind whether they have the 'It' factor or not. 'Once a music director came to me with a tune. Within thirty seconds, I knew it wasn't for me and I told him to stop. He complained, "Aapne to mukhda bhi nahin suna" [You haven't even heard the opening refrain]. So I told him, "Even thirty seconds of my life are very precious, I can't let you waste them. It is another matter that I may spend five hours explaining to you why I didn't like your thirty seconds of music, but that's my prerogative."'

Equally, there is a long line of actors he has benignly patronized despite repeated flops. They're mostly women like Antara Mali and Nisha Kothari, with whom he has been linked romantically (that's a debatable word with Ramu, but more on that subsequently), but also male stars like Abhishek Bachchan and Riteish Deshmukh—both men with powerful fathers.

Is that what he meant by sex and power being the only two realities in life, I wondered. With Vilasrao, Riteish Deshmukh's father, he played a memorable role in pruning some of the former chief minister's pelf. Vilasrao Deshmukh had to step down after the furore that followed his visit to the destroyed wing of the Taj Mahal Hotel during the 26/11 terror attacks in the company of Ramu and Riteish.

Simmering public ire over the insensitivity of politicians boiled over at what seemed like an actor and director's recce trip for a film, that too at a time when Mumbai was still traumatized. Punsters immediately jumped into the act as Vilasrao Deshmukh was forced to abdicate his post. 'Ramu ne do *Sarkar* banai, aur ek girayi.' It's the kind of gallows humour he appreciates.

'I was supposed to meet Riteish at his home that morning for some work. When he asked me if I wanted to accompany his dad for a tour of the Taj, I said yes. Is there anyone who would have said no to such an invite?' he responded mildly.

Though he moved to Mumbai in the early nineties to make *Rangeela,* a candyfloss romance, Ramu has been entranced by Mumbai's underbelly. The same curiosity that landed him at the Taj Mahal Hotel also led him to underworld informers, encounter cops, and hardened IPS officers. He has since become cinema's equivalent of an ambulance chaser, its tabloid hack. 'To me, this sleazy

Mumbai appears like a fairyland,' he said, 'and I am like the kid in that fairyland—everything about it excites my interest.'

He recalled his first ever flight into Mumbai. 'As the aircraft readied to land, I was astonished to see the shanties of Dharavi. From the air, it seemed as if there were a million homes under one continuous roof.' That impression was to have the most unlikely resonance. In his slick underworld film, *Company*, he used a chase through the slums, shot extensively from top angle. A similar sequence was used by one-time Ramu acolyte Anurag Kashyap in *Black Friday*, his cinematic recreation of the 1993 Mumbai blasts—which inspired Danny Boyle to open his *Slumdog Millionaire* with a memorable sequence shot in Dharavi itself.

It's fashionable to trash Ramu's recent films, as it should be given his fall (the film critic Mayank Shekhar calls his new work V-grade cinema) but Ram Gopal Varma captured the anomie of urban life, the thrum of anxiety that underlies life in the big city before anyone else did. 'All my life I had lived in a bungalow in Hyderabad; I experienced the curious world of the apartment for the first time when I came to Mumbai. Just a one-foot-thick wall, sometimes not even that, separates us from the intimacy of the other, and yet there is such alienation. The idea of *Satya* came to me from something a friend of mine had told me. He used to live in a seventeen-storey high-rise in Oshiwara. Off and on he would bump into this man in the car park or the elevator. They would exchange a hello, hi and go their own way. Then one day my friend's wife read in the papers that this very man had committed murder back in his hometown, and the police had finally traced him to Mumbai, and arrested him. I was chilled by the account, and it became the starting point for the story of this simple girl who unwittingly falls in love with the gangster, Satya.'

The bare apartment—with a dominant poster of Aishwarya Rai on the wall and a single mattress on the floor—is as much a character in *Not a Love Story* as Emile or Maria or Neeraj. That it was shot in Dheeraj Solitaire in the flat above 201-B, where Neeraj was killed and dismembered without anyone suspecting anything amiss, adds to the eeriness—and also the cheesiness—of the narrative.

After living in one apartment block for almost twenty years, time enough for a generation to grow up and be gone, Ramu would be hard-pressed to recognize anyone from his housing society. What he does recognize astutely are the changes sweeping through India's urban society, the rapidly shifting sexual mores, and the altering equation between men and women, with technology as the catalyst.

With great candour, he lists himself as a test case. Long separated from his wife, he has enjoyed a string of liaisons, but says he enjoys his freedom far too much to ever get into a deeper emotional commitment. 'But there's no one in this world who loves women more than I do. If I am attracted to someone I come right out and say, "I'd rather have sex with you than conversation."

'Traditionally,' he continued, spilling his seduction secrets, 'women want to be loved for everything except their bodies. But really! Should I love you for your handicrafts or that Fabindia kurta or for your mind? I once told an actress who wanted to come to my house for a business meeting, "By all means come, but if you do I'll have to first kiss you, else I'll be distracted all through, and the meeting would have been a waste.'" Charm may be at a premium, but his strike rate, he assured me cockily, is 'a hundred percent'. We don't pursue this line of conversation further but later, going through his tweets—he tweets as compulsively as he shoots movies—I find more of Ramu's expositions on women: 'I any day prefer a vodka drunkenness to a womans wakefulness' [sic]. And then again: 'Women nd God are two things I love to talk about becos I hate both of them.' He finds the sexuality of porn actresses liberating as they come 'completely edited and also with a remote control'. In *Not a Love Story*, the woman inspired by Maria is blemishless. Neeraj's character is vapid, a Mr goody-two-shoes, swiftly done away with, while Ramu has veered the farthest for Emile's character, showing him to be a near-psychotic lover. What remains with the audience after the hurried-through ending is the camera, like the director's eye, forever darting, resting sometimes on the heroine's breast, between her legs, on her bare arm, caressing her derrière. In his film Ram Gopal Varma made no moral judgement about Maria, seeing her as a sexual creature—edited and remote-controlled by him. Maria, her lawyer later told me, had refused to see the movie.

Book III

Death and Dénouement

7

Neeraj

'He was seemingly sweet, but the boy liked to play dangerous games.'

—Ekta Kapoor

Neeraj's online avatar was 'Rebel' and he described his passions as 'nethn [anything] dat involves adventure... risk b it @ work or in life'. Asked to describe his favourite activities, he wrote in his profile, 'wat kinna activities r v talking about???'

Good question.

His relationship status said, 'Committed', prompting a friend, presumably a woman, to expostulate in a flurry of red and blue emoticons. 'You are committed!!! Kuttey, Kaminey...' before lapsing into that feminine endearment of helpless love, 'Doggggggie.'

More than a year after his death, Neeraj's friends had kept his Orkut account alive. From fond reminiscences to hysterical exhortations for Neeraj to 'come back', the scraps were a vivid account of his friendships.

There was Priyanka writing: 'v heard dat news dat u r no more its been a yr . . . . bt idiot still i wud reqst u to cm bck ginni . . . . i wil slap u . . . . . . jaldi aao.wat r u testng??? bolo . . . . kb aaoge? ?????????????????????
??
???'

Another friend, Virat Bhargava, wrote: 'Neeraj bhai. . . i ve got married, tu tou nahi aaya. . .busy hai kya kahi. . .? itni bhi kya jaldi thi bhai jaane ki. . .miss u a lot. . .rest in peace.' (You didn't come for my marriage, are you that busy . . . how could you leave us so soon.)

And then there was someone who identified themselves as Maverick: 'Used to hate you. . . . . .i still do. . .really hate you neeraj grover. . .still. . .i do not like the way ur life ended. . .it was cruel and i wish ur soul rests in peace. . . but mind you. . .i still hate you.'

For these friends, most of whom kept in touch only virtually, Neeraj's online presence was a pleasant deception. In this floating space we are all eternal. But away from Orkut, Neeraj had another cyber identity on Yahoo Messenger as Karan Oberoi, where he described himself as the scion of Oberoi and Oberoi Constructions. It helped that there is a multi-million dollar real estate company in Mumbai called Oberoi Constructions. 'He thought the name Karan Oberoi had a posh ring to it, and it would help him snare girls,' said his friend 'J'. 'I can vouch that it worked for him, too.'

J, who did not want to be identified, was a close friend of Neeraj's at Amity University at Noida, and had preceded him to Mumbai to work in television. On the day of Rakesh Maria's press conference, he was in Kanpur and saw the news of Neeraj's killing on television. 'I had known he was missing,' he said, 'but about his death, that's where I heard it first.'

Aside from grief there was the shock of recognition. 'I had once told him that if he continued to behave the way he did, he would go to hell.' But that was an innocuous phrase, I said offering consolation. Shorn of venom, the words were just things friends said to each other. For instance, there was another friend of theirs from Amity, a young woman called Mona, who had this to say about Neeraj on Orkut: 'O ma god d guy who luks lyk a bhoot n druggy. . .no sense of humour, shameless, duffer, mad, etc etc etc etc. . .v were 2gether in coll bt v hardly had a wrd wid eachodr I gotto knw him in our coll fest whr I startd tlkin to dis duffr. . .hes gem of a prsn. . .I wish his aall dreamz may cum true n plz god giv him 1 single gal in lyf. . .always looks for new pataka around. . .hes a big kamina in dat case. . .'

Pretty fine testimonial, I thought. 'You don't understand.' J was not amused by my attempts to soothe him. 'When I said he'd go to hell, I had MEANT it.'

Our fascination with the criminal mind is such that we often associate the crime with the perpetrator, seldom the victim. Recall the famous Nanavati murder case of 1959, several incorrect parallels to which had been drawn with this case. In that murder a naval officer, Kawas Nanavati, discovered that his wife, an Englishwoman named Sylvia, was having an affair. In a fit of jealous rage Nanavati shot dead her lover while he lay in the bathtub. It was the cause célèbre of its time, and even turned into a film called *Yeh Raaste Hain Pyar Ke*. But few people today remember the name of the victim, Prem Ahuja, a South Mumbai businessman. The tragedy of Neeraj's killing had been overtaken by a fascination with Maria Susairaj and the naval officer invariably described as 'dashing'. It was as if by dying, the young television executive wrote himself out of the story.

Five months after his death, I travelled to Kanpur to find out more about who Neeraj was, and what his world was like.

'The first STD call in India was made from Kanpur,' Shaad Ali told me. It's the sort of trivia entire generations learnt by rote, reading *Competition Success Review*. But the film director, no contender for the Civils, was using the fact to explain Kanpur's 'no-culture culture'.

After his parents divorced, Shaad moved to Kanpur with his mother, the communist leader Subhashini Ali, to live with his grandmother Captain Lakshmi Sahgal, a leading member of the Indian National Army and a close associate of Netaji Subhas Chandra Bose.

Kanpur, he said, became his refuge in the interim between 'getting into trouble' at Lawrence School, Sanawar, and the Welham Boys' School. 'Lucknow is just 83 kilometres away, separated by the river, but none of the nawabi tehzeeb impinged on Kanpur's consciousness. We have our "own-bred" milieu, and are not ashamed of it. If anything, Kanpurias have the chaap of not being easily impressed.'

The city's jugaadu, can-do spirit, and at the same time its insularity, inform Shaad's 2005 hit film, *Bunty Aur Babli*, a hi-jinks caper about two youngsters desperately looking to flee the claustrophobia of their small-town existence, to seek fame and the good life at any cost. It represented the ambition, the ennui, and the sense of entitlement of the post-1980s' generation, and their efforts to escape their constricting lives.

Three years after they crushed the Mutiny of 1857 and established Cawnpore as a garrison town, the colonial British set up the Harness and Saddlery Factory here to supply leather to the army across the country and then Cooper Allen and Co., which manufactured blankets for the army. The textile behemoths, Elgin Mills and Muir Mills, followed soon after. Kanpur, smug in its prosperity, positioned itself as the 'Manchester of the East'.

After Independence, the seths took over the mills, and old families like the Kejriwals, the Singhanias, and the Jaipurias added sugar and gutka factories, textile and steel mills to Kanpur's industrial growth. The leather and autoparts industry flourished, and mimicking its British past, the owners of Lal Imli Woollens built a replica of the Big Ben to ring in the hour. 'Till the 1960s there was a huge administrative upper class in Kanpur that kept out the others, much like the British did,' said Shaad's mother Subhashini Ali.

Her own family's trajectory seems twined to the fortunes of the city. Subhashini's parents, Captain Lakshmi and Colonel Prem Sahgal, were both members of the Indian National Army. In 1945, Prem Sahgal was arrested by the British for abetting the Japanese. Prem, along with two other men, a Muslim, Shah Nawaz Khan, and a Sikh, Gurdial Singh, was subjected to a public trial at the Red Fort.

'The accused, by virtue of the fact that they represented the three major religious communities, enjoyed a huge tidal wave of public support,' wrote Subhashini in her family account. The British were forced to eventually pardon the three. However, Prem, public hero or not, found himself unemployable. At the behest of a swadeshi mill owner, he and Lakshmi moved to make Kanpur their home.

By the time Subhashini, their card-carrying Marxist daughter, represented the city as its Member of Parliament in 1991, Kanpur was in the midst of the most tumult it had known since the British takeover. Administrative neglect, a series of communal riots and violent industrial lockouts precipitated its drop from India's sixth largest town to ninth and then tenth. As the obsolete textile mills quavered to a halt, the Manchester of the East was left just East of Manchester. A purposeless young generation, unable to find a place in the city's working culture, found an outlet in the growing Hindutva movement which was to peak in 1992 with the destruction of the Babri Masjid in neighbouring Ayodhya.

Because of its colonial past and excellent educational institutions, Kanpur saw itself as a big city, but its physical reality no longer supported the aspirations and ambitions of its young. 'As the nucleus of the city disappeared—industrial production dropped, the grain and cloth markets moved away—so did its talent,' said Subhashini Ali.

Writers and intellectuals shifted to Mumbai to work in the film industry, or to academia in Delhi, leaving behind a largely mercantile culture. Other than malls, multiplexes, food, gossip, and ostentatious weddings, the city had little to offer by way of a productive life. 'Don't forget to mention the jagrans, we're big on jagrans,' she added.

Subhashini had since faded into the fringes of electoral politics, and went on to head the All India Democratic Women's Association (AIDWA); her mother, the ninety-plus Lakshmi, a doctor by training, continued her practice in the city. Shaad had moved to Mumbai, where he spun shiny yarns that lured young people like Neeraj from all over the country.

When it dawned on him that he was expected to sit at the dukaan, and in the not-so-distant future take over the running of the family's thriving photocopying shop on Mall Road, Neeraj Grover felt the kick of desperation. His life would not echo his father's. He rebelled. 'I will achieve something, I will become someone,' he shot back at his mother each time the subject of the shop came up.

'Yeh kahaan se upper class bachcha paida kiya hai?' (Where have we produced this upper class child from?) Amarnath Grover often despaired to his wife. Perhaps it was their fault, sending him to Jaipuria High School, where the kids of Kanpur's 'cream class' studied, the children of bureaucrats and businessmen. For Neeraj was shaukeen like no one else in the family. He would only fly, refusing to take trains when they travelled. He insisted on wearing international brands, dismissing local companies as producing 'sastaa maal', and patronized Profile, Kanpur's most expensive hair salon, where he paid Rs 500 for a trim. 'I have not paid that much for all my haircuts put together through my entire life,' Amarnath Grover complained. But he always gave his son the money.

At school, Neeraj was for the most part an average student. When his mother would ask him how he had fared in his exams, he'd say, not always in jest, 'I wrote down everything that my neighbour knew.' But after his indifferent degree in commerce from Christchurch College, during which he also assisted his father with the business, Neelam Grover noticed a change in her son. 'I could sense his frustration, his desperation to get out of Kanpur. He took career counselling, started looking up all sorts of advertisements and taking entrance tests.' During this time he read in the local youth paper, *Josh*, about a degree in mass media and applied for it at Jamia Millia and Amity in Noida. He qualified for both but chose Amity, a private university which has skilfully marketed itself as an institution aspiring to international standards. Certainly, the fees at Rs 9 lakh for the two-year course, was on dollar parity. Against their better judgement, overriding financial constraints, and fighting every protective impulse, the Grovers agreed to fund the course at Amity.

I travelled to Kanpur by car from Lucknow, crossing the Ganga spread out like a creased sari on the river bed. A little over an hour later I was in the city, lost in the maze of the many nagars—Dada Nagar, Govind Nagar, Nirala Nagar, Kidwai Nagar. Finally Saket Nagar, where past the mounds of sand and cement and the unfinished buildings, I finally found Ma Saraswati Apartments. Having sold their largish single-storey bungalow because they were going to relocate to Mumbai to be with Neeraj, the Grovers had now shifted into a flat. The building was still under construction, but they had no option but to move in.

The Grovers, who had shifted just two days before I visited, were already known in the neighbourhood as the family that had been marked by tragedy. Though they had not entirely settled in yet, the kitchen was fully functional. There was the ceremony of the visiting journalist—chai, nashta, the old-world courtesy that would not permit resentment at the intrusion; in fact the extended family had been invited for lunch so that everyone could talk about Neeraj.

Neelam Grover handled everything with efficiency. I got my tea, and at last she sat down, wiping sweat off her face with the edge of her synthetic sari. It was a mild October day and not that warm, but her blouse was saturated.

'Neeraj and I spoke to each other at least twice a day. He would tell us everything about his life...' she tapered off, 'Except about Maria.'

Just fifty-five, her neck had wrinkled like the folds of a collapsed accordion, as if the battle to hold her head up had been surrendered. A deep groove ran down the centre of her forehead. She rattled off facts about her son mechanically. The year he was born (1983); his educational background; what kind of a boy he was—'Loving, fun, funny, very close to the family, dog lover...' She sat straight, then sideways, shifting on the sofa, first away from me then towards me. Her restless grief wouldn't allow her to be still. It would not have been out of place if she had suddenly let out a primordial scream.

Amarnath Grover's family had migrated to Kanpur from Bannu, near Peshawar in West Pakistan, during Partition. He married Neelam in 1979 and the couple had two children, a girl and a boy in quick succession, both of whom inherited their mother's good looks.

While Neelam stayed put in Kanpur with her in-laws and the children, Amarnath Grover travelled around the country for his job as an officer with the Cotton Corporation of India. He took voluntary retirement in 1988 and returned to Kanpur to set up a successful stationery and photocopy shop in the city's business centre.

Travel can either liberate you, or bind you closer to home. Amarnath Grover's years of living alone and moving around the country had produced in him a wariness of the world and a mistrust of ambition. He could not understand his young son's desire to leave Kanpur, or his abhorrence for managing the shop. 'I had to, at the age of forty, wash my own clothes, survive on paani-waale aaloo, and spend solitary evenings staring out of the window; it was not pleasant. I wanted to spare Ginni all that,' he said; his gaunt face and thin flanks marking him out as much older than his fifty-nine years.

Like the young prince Siddharth's parents, who tried to defy prophecy by creating an idyll for their son within their palace, Amarnath Grover strove to bring the world to Neeraj. Whatever he wished for, Neeraj got. Whether it was a kennel for his pet Silky, a Rs 35,000 Nikon though Neeraj had precious little to do with photography, expensive clothes, a motorbike, a car. 'He was a demanding kid. I remember we bought him an LML Freedom, but within six months an upgraded bike—Bajaj Pulsar—was launched. He then wanted that,' said Neelam. Resolved not to let his son step out of his radius, and perhaps guilty for it, the father succumbed to each demand.

'Main uski aankh tarasti nahin dekh sakta tha' (I couldn't see him want for anything), he said.

Often this came at the cost of their own desires. 'Kai baar apna man dabaa ke Ginni ki ichcha poori ki' (Often we sacrificed our own desires to fulfil his wants), said Neelam. Of the two she appeared more realistic in her assessment of their son.

As his father's life got smaller, and his love more suffocating, Neeraj's resolve to leave Kanpur strengthened. The offer from Amity was his key to escape. Father and son played out an old game—Neeraj demanded, and Amarnath Grover conceded. The one thing he had tried to prevent all these years had come to pass. The opening act of the tragedy was laid out.

Jolly, clever, and helpful are words that are used without exception to describe Neeraj by everyone I spoke to. Hitank, his junior at Amity, who is now based in Mumbai, and was at the Grovers for lunch during my visit, reminisced, 'On my first day away from home, I got lost in Delhi. I had to meet my mother some place, but I had neither the address nor a phone. Neeraj bhai, a stranger then, stayed with me for four hours helping me locate her.'

The two young men went on to become roommates and firm friends over the next two years. 'He was protective of me, easy-going, and he cracked terrible PJs. Because of all his qualities he was a big hit with the girls too.'

Since this was being said in the presence of Neeraj's parents, Hitank measured his words but conceded that Neeraj was a bit of an attention seeker—'but in a nice way'. 'He couldn't bear to be alone and was forever looking for company. He was particular about the good life, and his quota of partying. He loved to eat chicken momos, the shawarma at Al-Bake at New Friends. Even developed a bit of a tummy though he was only twenty-four. We used to joke that there was a little Gautam growing inside.'

Neeraj also insisted on maintaining his own living space, despite spending most of his time in a privately run hostel with Hitank and his friends. 'I often told him that he should let me manage his money since he squandered it, but he would say that at no cost would he compromise on his lifestyle.'

During vacations, when he was not going home to Kanpur, Neeraj tried his hand at multiple jobs—hawking a newly launched mobile phone at shopping malls, event management, working with the audience research cell at NDTV, where his brief was to get and manage the audience for various shows. 'He was even-tempered, hard-working, and quick on his feet; but he wasn't focused, and he couldn't last anywhere for too long,' said Hitank. 'He was preoccupied with becoming rich and famous somehow.' He uncannily shared these traits with Maria. She too flitted from one thing to another, incapable of staying the course in either Bangalore or Mumbai.

Given his ambition, it was natural that Neeraj would gravitate to Mumbai, arriving in the city towards the end of 2006. The quicksilver world of television suited his personality. Over the next year and a half Neeraj changed five jobs, averaging roughly four months at each. He had joined Siddharth Basu's Synergie Adlabs just a week before he was killed.

Though he himself has stayed put with one production house for almost six years, Deepak Kumar, Neeraj's fellow Coffee House Nomad and relationship troubleshooter, termed these jumps as 'normal' in the television industry. 'Neeraj was sharp, hard-working, and responsible the minute he reached the sets. If he put in four hours and someone else put in eight, they would get the same results. He always moved jobs for better money or greater responsibility at work. He was very clear about what he wanted—fame, money, and pretty girls. Our ultimate aspiration was to be like Vijay Mallya. We wanted the yachts and the models floating around us.'

Back in Kanpur the Grovers were delighted with Ginni's progress and increments, seeing nothing amiss with his rapid job changes. 'The feeling these days is that the golden opportunity must be taken, whatever the cost,' said Crime Branch chief Rakesh Maria. 'Salary has become the new yardstick of value. As children come into their own considerable money, parents don't care about much else. Look at Maria Susairaj, she was staying with different boys when she came to Mumbai. I remember when I went to Delhi for my UPSC exams my dad called his friends to come and pick me up and made sure that I stayed with them, and I was a guy. Children these days have become like gladiators, left to deal with the beasts on their own.'

Independence and early affluence can also inhibit parents from speaking their mind to their children. Add to that the sense of spurious intimacy created by the speed-dial button. The Grovers, who spoke to Neeraj twice a day, were lulled into a false comfort that they knew everything that was going on in their son's life. They listened to his words, yet were unable to read his voice—caught up in the superficialities of Hello, How are you? How was your day, dear?

It was his friends in Delhi and Mumbai who had a better measure of Neeraj. And one of the things they all speak about is his fascination with women. 'When he disappeared and we started looking for him, girlfriends turned up like finds at an excavation at Mohenjodaro,' said Nishant Lal.

'He made women feel very comfortable, which is why they trusted him and were drawn to him, but Neeraj could also spontaneously switch from one woman to another without wasting much emotion,' added Deepak Kumar. 'Once the relationship was over he would just text or call them and say that they were through, and that he did not want to meet them again. Or, I would have to field their calls during the transition phase and make excuses on his behalf. We had a whole list of them. I did occasionally get the feeling that some of these women were emotionally involved, which is why they gave of themselves to him.'

J, who perhaps saw Neeraj most closely in Delhi, and loved him as a brother, had this to say: 'He was terribly insecure and was always trying to prove that he had achieved something. This extended to his relationships with women as well. He tried his luck with every girl he met. He was also very open about his relationships. So, if he met a new girl, he would talk candidly about his past girlfriends with her, including the ones who had dumped him.'

'By doing so he conveyed that he was transparent and open, and women would love him for that. He was a very good player. His problem was that while he could dump all the girls he wanted to, his behaviour would turn self-destructive if some woman were to do the same to him. He would bitch her out, saying things like, 'I am much better looking, us bandi ka boyfriend is so ordinary, she has no class,' and so on. When his first girlfriend in Delhi left him, he took to drinking heavily and bad-mouthed her everywhere. It became a pattern with him.

'But he also had great charm, I have seen him pick up girls just standing on the road, or at a market in Malviya Nagar. He hardly studied while at Amity; most of his projects would be done by some girl or the other. Often he would pick up very plain-looking or even downright ugly girls and chat them up.'

However, both J, who vouched for Neeraj's excellent professional reputation, and Deepak Kumar emphatically refuted rumours of Neeraj abusing his position as associate creative director at Balaji Telefilms to seek sexual favours from aspirants like Maria Susairaj.

'He was charming, he didn't need to resort to that. Also, there are about a thousand assistant creative heads in TV in Mumbai, Neeraj was one of them. All he could do was pass on the aspirants' audition tapes to his superior in the production house or to the channel; he did not have the clout to cast someone.'

'Though,' Deepak Kumar said after a pause, 'he was a big mouth, and could convey the wrong impression. We went to Goa in December 2007 where he had a drag from a joint and he pretended for the whole day as if he was high. If he went to a nightclub at Andheri, he would boast that he had gone to a swishier one in South Mumbai. He was good at that, but we, his friends, always knew when he was being a cartoon network.' Perhaps it was this boasting that led Maria to later claim that Neeraj was into drugs. Save for the odd experimentation there was no evidence to suggest that he ever did so.

Ekta Kapoor, Neeraj's boss at Balaji where he put in his longest stint, was characteristically more forceful. 'He was a wasted little boy!' She waved her bejewelled hand in an expansive, dismissive sweep. 'After he quit us I learnt he used to go around boasting about his proximity to me. He was a cute boy, smart, smooth operator who talked too much. A couple of times I had to tell him to keep his mouth shut. But he wasn't a bad sort and in my presence he would sit quietly, legs crossed demurely like a bride, which is why,' she said chuckling with the relish of a born gossip, 'I was really surprised to know that he had a reputation as something of a stud.'

During his five-month stay at Balaji, Neeraj was involved in successive relationships with three of his colleagues. He wriggled out of one of them by telling the woman that being with her was making him forget a former girlfriend who'd died, which in turn made him feel unfaithful! 'Later we found out he had a dog who'd died, but never a girlfriend. Ha ha ha. . .' Ekta doubled up in laughter but was quick to sober down. 'He was seemingly sweet, but the boy liked to play dangerous games,' she remarked perceptively. 'He often hit on women whom he knew to be already involved. It was some kind of a sexual power trip for him, and many guys hated him for that.'

One of these relationships turned sour for Neeraj after the woman scorned was promoted as his boss at Balaji. She began to keep tabs on his work. And the one time he tripped up, trying to pass off some old audition tapes for *Mahabharat* (the same serial for which he had auditioned Maria Susairaj) as fresh ones, she alerted Ekta Kapoor. When the woman with the most feared temper in the entertainment industry was told she was being fooled, she put him on a deadline of one night to rustle up eighty fresh auditions. Neeraj chose the easier option. He found another job.

Only once, says Deepak Kumar, did he see Neeraj distraught over a woman. 'She was a common friend'—the one he had given the fake engagement ring to. 'He thought she was two-timing him with her old boyfriend.' After a public blow-up with her he retreated into a sulk and even wrote some maudlin lyrics:

Dil phir kyon itna bechain hai
Phir sookhe mere ye nain hain
Dil janta hai tu kahan mere pas hai
Phir bhi ek kasak na
Jaane kyon bechain hai...
(Why is the heart so restless,
and my eyes bereft of tears.
You're not near me and yet
I feel a twinge. Why this restlessness,
I know not)

'I cheered him up by setting it to music,' said Sushant, Neeraj's music director flatmate. 'Neeraj, Haresh and I sat till 3 am making a scratch recording. It was the most fun we've had. Neeraj had the talent to become a sensitive lyric writer.' Sushant plugged in his keyboard in the living room and played the melody for me. After he'd bounced back from the break-up, Neeraj would often get women friends to the flat and ask Sushant to play 'merawala song'. Sushant said he was now in talks with Sonu Nigam to get him to sing it in Neeraj's memory.

Of all his friends and family only Haresh Sondarva, his other flatmate, picked on the strains of Neeraj's fixation with women. 'His obsession with girls was a sickness. He never wanted to be alone, and he couldn't bear to be without a girl for long. If we were a group of guys watching a film or just hanging out, Neeraj would be there with us but he'd get bored after a while and call a woman friend over.'

The fashion designer, twenty-nine, who shared, and just as often not, the room with Neeraj, says he never asked him why he brought so many women home. 'Somebody had to adjust, and it was always me.' But he did get a good sense of Neeraj's problem. 'Once he took Ecstasy after which he told me that the drug's impact lasted on him for two or three days. For the first time, he said to me, I feel relaxed and I am not constantly thinking of women, it's such a relief.'

After Neeraj's death, Haresh along with Neeraj's cousin conducted a small shanti path for him. They packed some of his belongings and brought them to the Versova beach where, amidst the waves dissolving by their feet, producing that strangely intimate sound, they immersed Neeraj's belongings, and offered a prayer to the retreating sun. Neeraj's cousin told Haresh, 'We had come to Mumbai with such hopes but what have we ended with?'

Shattered by the tragedy the small group has since disintegrated. Neeraj's cousin has moved to Delhi, the woman Neeraj introduced to his parents as the one he wanted to marry has gone back to her hometown unable to deal with either Neeraj's betrayal with Maria or his killing, and Haresh himself is looking to leave. 'This city is so inhumane. Have you tried boarding the local train? You may—if you struggle long enough—get somewhere here, but you lose a lot in the bargain. There's no breathing space. It affects your mental health,' he said intensely, still deeply affected by the events.

'After Neeraj's death I came to realize the unethical things that go on in the name of so-called modernity. I have begun to question all that.' Several months later when I called Haresh to check a quote he told me he had relocated to Pune and was the happier for it.

Shaken by the tragedy, one of Neeraj's women friends too offered a public forgiveness, writing on his wall: 'I didn't know the last time I saw you would be The Last Time I'd ever get to see you. . . I pray and hope that your mom and dad gather the strength required to sail through this fierce storm. All this is still so unbelievable. Violence to this extreme? I don't understand how their [criminals'] conscience would have allowed them to lie and live even if they'd never been caught. May you be blessed with Moksha. You weren't a bad man, Neeraj, you didn't deserve this. Not an early death, and not a disgraceful end.'

Even though there was some laughter, thanks to their grandchildren, it would take a long time for peace and happiness to find a place in the Kanpur home of the Grovers. It was a full house the day I visited. Shikha was there with her two children and husband. Neelam Grover's brother Satnam Arora, the family's steadiest support in those dark days when Neeraj was missing, was present with his wife and teenaged daughter, as was Amarnath Grover's sister-in-law, whose son had lived with Neeraj in Mumbai.

There was plenty of chatter, the scraping of spoon against plate, and the gurgle of young children being tickled by their Naanu. But the skein of grief ran thick.

Amarnath Grover moved around the house a diminished man, shorn of the light of life. There's an untranslatable word in Hindi for it, shree-heen. His wife's eyes tailed him anxiously. 'He's so distracted, forgetful,' she complained to her sisters-in-law as he moved out of earshot. 'He goes to get dahi, will pay for it but forget the packet. He'll see a boy of Ginni's age on the road and start to cry. I have forbidden him from driving the scooter because his eyes well up. Then he can't see and may have an accident.' The family has now hired a driver for the white Santro they had bought for Neeraj after he passed out of school.

'For twenty years he never missed opening the shutters of the shop at 8.30 am sharp,' Neelam Grover turned around to tell me. 'But now, he just doesn't want to leave the house, or he'll go really late. Some boys are running it indifferently. When I chide him he finds excuses and then says, who should I go for now? What is the point?' Her face crumpled as she spoke.

Later when he and I were out of the house, Amarnath Grover said he'd stopped going to the shop because he didn't want to leave Neelam all by herself in the house. 'God knows what all she will keep thinking. As it is she has lost so much weight, become half of her size.'

It was here, in this simple home, in this unremarkable town, where the high-decibel big-city case distilled into the purest tragedy for an ageing man and his wife.

But it was more than the loss of a beautiful, vibrant son; it was the promise of his future cut short that had broken the Grovers. To use a phrase from Kafka in an altogether different context, Neeraj's death had hit Amarnath Grover like an ice-axe that broke the frozen sea inside his soul. This is what psychotherapists call the onset of awareness. As the shards disintegrated and collapsed, so did his notions about his perfect son. On more than one occasion through that day he had asked if I had, during my interviews for this book, learnt anything adverse about Neeraj.

On one occasion, an aunt interjected, sailing into hyperbole. 'What's there to ask? Itna seedha bachcha tha, working hard all the time [He was such a simple child]. Kabhi naa smoke naa drink [Never smoked or drank]. In our family toh bachche call and complain [In our family, kids call and complain], how come you never taught us any wiles, how are we to deal with this world?'

But Amarnath Grover continued to look searchingly, expectantly, as if he already knew something and now only needed corroboration. What could I tell the grieving father? 'Nothing unusual, except for the women,' I offered weakly. 'Oh, that we know about!' Shikha and the cousin let out a gust of relief. 'He was so good-looking and the TV industry is full of girls.'

'Especially in production, there are no handsome boys,' Amarnath Grover spoke up slowly. 'You know, while he was still studying in Kanpur,' he said, 'Ginni had a friend and one day he brought her to the shop. This girl, well, she came in wearing tight jeans and a T-shirt, her hair was shorter than mine. I told Neeraj, do you think someone like her can really take care of you? Believe me; from the next day on he stopped meeting her. That way he was very obedient. He wanted to marry a homely girl.'

'It's our misfortune that he got entangled with that chudail.' Neelam Grover was sobbing inconsolably now. 'The way they cut up his body, we didn't even get anything to perform last rites to. That's not like the behaviour of human beings, is it?'

'These girls...' Amarnath Grover clamped up abruptly. 'Beta, what's your name?'

'Meenal.'

'Hahn, okay. You know these type of girls from that community'—I realized as he went on that he had asked my name to check my religious identity—'are all like that. I also found out from a TV reporter that Maria has a friend called Ejaz. You must investigate if there's an underworld nexus.' In this moment of crazed grief, long-held prejudices had unmoored and surfaced.

Amarnath Grover wanted to show me his shop before I left Kanpur. I got the sense that he wanted to talk alone, away from the family. But in the car for the most part he was quiet, looking out of the window, exhausted by his catharsis. He broke the silence only to ask again, strangely insistent, 'Have you heard anything bad about Neeraj? Because if you have, tell us, we must know.'

But I had no revelations to make.

The shop was redolent with the smell of photocopy ink, and doing brisk business despite the patina of neglect. 'We've added a few computers so it can also double up as a cyber café. Recently I sat down and put together Neeraj's papers and investments, it totalled Rs 17 lakh. All that and this.' He waved a hand around, his face full of strain, overrunning with tears. 'This shop, it was his. Isn't this world enough?'

8

The Unravelling

'The fact is that the crime is never perfect.'

—Jean Baudrillard

Details of the material evidence recovered and recorded by the Crime Branch during their investigation were like a Mensa puzzle. All the clues to Neeraj's killing—the method and also the malevolence—lay in these items:

1. One bone, one foot long, burnt on one side.
2. Remnants of a burnt bag, red in colour.
3. Reddish-coloured half-burnt cloth.
4. Burnt pillow, pillowcase, burnt cloth, and plastic piece, all red.
5. One white metal chain with small beads found in a burnt and broken condition.

6. Half-burnt yellow metal chain with a pendant designed like an elephant head.
7. A small broken bottle of perfume.
8. A bottle of deodorant with burn marks.
9. A thin white plastic bottle found in smashed condition.
10. Coins, chain lock, metal buttons from clothing, all recovered in a blackened state.
11. Sticks, stones, ash mixed with earth.
12. Sample of earth recovered from the jungles of Manor.
13. Sample of a scraping of kitchen wall from flat number 201, Dheeraj Solitaire in Malad.
14. Control scraping of colour from the same kitchen wall.
15. Sample of blood found in the rose-coloured curtain in the bedroom of flat 201, Dheeraj Solitaire, Malad.
16. Sample of blood from the outer latch of the bedroom.
17. Sample of blood from the television speaker in the bedroom.
18. Sample of blood from a patterned green-and-white pillow cover.
19. Bloodstained blue jeans with the label Skinny on the inside.
20. A pair of women's size 5 Nike shoes found with faint blood-like stains.
21. A maroon-coloured half-sleeve XL-size T-shirt with the label Xylem.
22. One 13-inch chopper with an 8-inch-long blade recovered from the jungles of Manor.
23. A Santro car bearing the licence plate MH-04-BQ-9866.
24. Two black rexine covers from the back seat of the aforementioned car.

25. One black full mat and two foot mats recovered from the rear seat of the said car.
26. One rubber mat recovered from the boot of the said car.
27. Two pieces of sun-protection shield.
28. One parcel containing bones.
29. One 9-inch-long pointed tapering knife with a 5-inch blade with the following inscribed in English: Lord Stainless Steel.
30. One yellow-coloured 5-litre plastic can with the words: Saffola Losorb—The Heart Of A Family.
31. The cardboard packing of a 13-inch chopper and plastic cover. The content recorded on the packaging reads thus: SKU no. (Barcode no.) 100000432, bread knife LC0613-2LC. MRP all taxes Rs 265, Hypercity price Rs 179.
32. A silver and gold N-95 Nokia handset with the IMEI number 354835/01/278290/1 and sim card no. 8991920000080-656795 (belonging to Neeraj Grover).
33. A CD of accused Maria Susairaj's audition for the role of Draupadi for the serial *Mahabharat* produced by Balaji Telefilms.

These articles, neatly packed in an aluminium trunk, were court property, brought out occasionally to corroborate testimonies during a cross-examination, and opened barely a few feet away from where Maria Susairaj smiled sanguinely, and Emile Jerome stared grimly into the middle distance. Occasionally, a colourful plastic packet holding Neeraj's remains, or a bloodstained article would be unwrapped, releasing the dank and rancid odour of death. The entire courtroom recoiled visibly when this happened.

'Have you seen *Million Dollar Baby*? There's a great line in there. Clint Eastwood telling that girl Hillary Swank, who desperately wants to box: "No matter how good a fighter you are, you need to learn to defend yourself."'

Inspector Raorane never was a pugilist—volleyball was his preferred sport—but he liked to lie low; keep his guard up. The investigating officer in the Neeraj Grover case had been ducking my calls for weeks before finally agreeing to meet, on his first day off in a month, at the behest of Rakesh Maria. He called me to his office at the Maharashtra Housing Board (MHB) police station at Borivali, where among other things the inspector ensured communal peace, maintained a roster of duties, and solved routine cases of theft. He sought transfer from the high-profile Crime Branch to a police station after his wife fell ill. MHB, in the innards of Borivali, away from the glittering malls and glass-fronted buildings, was close to his home and saved him the commute.

The odd locations of police stations in Mumbai, and their varying stages of disrepair, merit a monograph if not a whole book. The Oshiwara police station, for instance, resembled Lego blocks assembled by a disinterested child. Wadala TT was situated in the middle—yes, smack in the middle—of busy railway tracks. Go complain at your own peril. Likewise Yellow Gate near the docks lay at the end of a deserted lane with no lights. At the Antop Hill police station the only drinking water available was from a filthy sink plumbed right at the door of an even filthier loo. When the promised land for their building failed to materialize, the cops at MHB, like their counterparts at Meghwadi, Bhandup, DN Nagar, Malvani, and Mulund, were instructed to set up the police station within their own living quarters.

It was a curious coexistence made unremarkable only by our acceptance of it. The sounds of an Ekta Kapoor serial pierced the thin walls of a sub-inspector's home and clashed with the piteous cries emanating from the detection room next door where the cops were probably interrogating a thief—doing their 'daily practice' in Inspector Raorane's euphemism. I made my way up the uneven steps—the grille of the lift was strangely mangled as if some mountain man had had a go at it—and bumped into a child running past the detention room for women prisoners. On the second floor, outside the home adjacent to the senior inspector's office, someone had painted an elaborate rangoli, signalling beauty in the midst of brutal harshness. That, it seemed to me, was one of the ways we coped in this manic city.

Inspector Raorane was a trim, energetic forty-five-year-old with a bushy moustache, marked by an alert, curious manner (he saw me scrawling my notes and wanted to know if I had learnt shorthand), but there was no denying the exhaustion that seemed to have seeped into the pores of his face, causing a slight puffiness. A few mounted photographs of him being felicitated by the then home minister R.R. Patil were the only concession to decoration in an otherwise bare, impersonal office equipped with a steel cupboard, a functional table, and two moulded plastic chairs.

'Did you hear of the famous heist at Joy Alukkas jewellers in Hyderabad?' he countered when I asked about the photographs. Some years ago Inspector Raorane, then posted at Dahisar with unit XII of the Crime Branch, was in his office surfing channels when he came across the news of the sensational robbery at Hyderabad's biggest jewellery store. As he watched the details emerge, a grin spread across the officer's face. The jewel thief's modus operandi bore the remarkable stamp of a man Inspector Raorane had been shadowing for a year, ever since his release from prison in Mumbai. His name was Vimal Rambali Singh, a man who, in Inspector Raorane's words was ugly as sin and sharper than a machete. 'I got on to the phone with an informer of mine who himself was a thief and who knew Singh,' he said. 'So, your chief has been hard at work, I told him.'

'We knew that Singh would have to come to Mumbai with his booty—he had cleared all the jewels from the heavily decked mannequins on the three floors of the store, not touching the vaults knowing well they'd have a more complex operating system [it was this strategy that had given him away to Inspector Raorane]. Only this city offers the anonymity where you can sell jewels worth six crore and no one will move a muscle.'

His hunch proved correct when Singh arrived in Mumbai within days of the heist. Inspector Raorane laid a trap for him at a restaurant at Bandra East. 'We got him but he didn't have the jewels on him, so we kept him in the office, confiscated his mobile, and waited. I knew if he didn't reach within a certain time, one of his associates would call and then we could trace that call. Our job was made easier when the associate called from a landline which belonged to a hotel in Grant Road.' In thirty-five minutes flat—he called it the most perilous journey of his life—Inspector Raorane and his team landed at the hotel. 'It was my lucky day. Just as we were going up the stairs to Singh's associate's room, we bumped into a man carrying a huge bag, heading out of the hotel. I don't know what instinct made me run to the reception and ask for that associate. The receptionist pointed at the man heading out. Had I postponed even by a couple of minutes, he would have just melted into Mumbai's crowd and also melted the jewels. This,' he said pointing to the pictures of the felicitation, 'was for that.'

The sharp sense of self he evinced came in part from his education. Inspector Raorane grew up in a tiny village, Navale, in Sindhudurg district, which had a population of less than five hundred, and where his father, now eighty-seven, was the local schoolteacher. Originally Sisodiyas from Udaipur, his ancestors got land in Sindhudurg in lieu of valorous services rendered. His maternal grandfather was in the police force in Mumbai during British rule. 'We are an educated family,' he said without emphasis, though the pride was unmistakable.

After school he moved to Kolhapur to study English literature. Why literature, I asked, intrigued by the detective's choice of subject. 'Because,' he said, taking his time to answer, '. . .literature keeps you alive. And that's true of it in any language. Look at P.L. Deshpande's work in Marathi, it's not just some comedy, he gives you a clear picture of what human beings are all about. Literature gives us perception.'

After completing an MA he joined the Ramakrishna Paramhans Mahavidyalaya at Osmanabad ('it had a great library') as the junior English lecturer. This was in 1984–5 when Rakesh Maria was also posted in the area as the Superintendent of Police (SP). 'My landlady had a dispute with her neighbour but she was a senior citizen who lived alone and had no one to help her, so I went along with her to meet the SP. He was most helpful and both of us came back quite impressed with his personality.'

Three years later some of his friends from Kolhapur persuaded him to appear for the Maharashtra Public Service Commission exam. 'Just like that—I was in my twenties, everything then seemed like a dare—I said okay.' He ranked fourteenth in the state and joined the police, even though the lecturer's pay was better and the job afforded him ample time to pursue interests like reading and volleyball. 'But this [policing] is the only job where you are in constant contact with the public and have the power to help.'

'Also,' he added with a hint of a smile, 'I now have a better appreciation of the angry ranting in *Paradise Lost*.'

Inspector Raorane's first posting was at Worli, where he moved in with his sister who lived next door to the police station. 'Her young children were very attached to me and often followed me into the police station, like these kids roaming here. But all day long they heard me shout or being rough, I didn't want them to see that, grow up to that, so I asked for a transfer to the traffic control branch.'

Here, he was to again meet Rakesh Maria, then the deputy commissioner of police. This was a little before the 1993 blasts when Maria got the lead to Tiger Memon and moved out of traffic to take over the blasts probe. 'Boss,' said Inspector Raorane admiringly, 'works with an inspector's instinct. He is not an ivory-tower man; he has great grasp of the grassroots as also a detective's skills.'

He himself picked up some of those during a stint with the Special Branch, which was considered a 'punishment posting' within the force as it entailed mostly paperwork, and almost no opportunity to skim cream. 'I once got an application for an arms licence; while checking the applicant's antecedents I found police files on his family dating back to the British. It was an instance of very fine record-keeping. I realized that's how those people were, meticulous, detailed, and mind you, this was before computers and typewriters. I was greatly inspired, thinking that if you are honest to your job this is how well you can do it.'

When Unit IX senior inspector Ashok Borkar returned from Rakesh Maria's office on the night of May 9 (hours after Amarnath Grover had met him) and told his men about a missing complaint that needed to be investigated, Inspector Raorane didn't pay much heed. 'I thought it was for someone else to follow.'

But as he lived closest to Malad where the missing complaint was registered—in this city of impossible traffic, that was an important consideration—he was nominated to lead the investigation. Helping him were the others in the unit: Assistant Inspector Sunil Ghosalkar, Sub-Inspectors Mahesh Tawade, Sagar Shivalkar, Sanjiv Gawade, Dilip Deshmukh, and Dilip Bhosle, Police Naik Nandkumar Naik, and Head Constable Sadanand Gurav. They were a fine mesh—each man bringing his own special skills to bear on the case eventually.

Borkar, who was proceeding on a brief vacation, warned Inspector Raorane before leaving, 'Boss is really keen to find out what happened to this guy.' Ghosalkar and Naik had already begun the hunt for Neeraj, accompanying Amarnath Grover to mortuaries, hospitals and even to the Borivali National Park. Inspector Raorane, still sceptical about what he could bring to the case, began with a visit to the Malad police station to get copies of any statements recorded. The case was still at an inquiry stage, and a senior IPS officer had already called the Malad police asking them to go slow on Maria.

Inspector Raorane saw that a missing complaint had been registered by Neeraj's cousin, and the police had recorded the statements of Neeraj's friends, among them Nishant Lal, as well as Emile Jerome and Maria Susairaj. Maria was the last recorded person to have seen the missing man. An FIR for kidnapping by unknown persons was eventually filed by Amarnath Grover only on May 20, when it seemed certain that something dire had happened to his son.

Neeraj, Maria had told the police, had come to her house after 10.30 pm on the night of May 6, but left at 1.30 am following several calls from his friends. One of these, she alleged, was from Nisha, a former colleague at Balaji Telefilms, who insisted that Neeraj come over, saying to him, 'Aa jao, naya maal aaya hai' (Come, fresh stuff is here). Maria was to later insinuate that Neeraj was hooked to recreational drugs.

Before leaving Dheeraj Solitaire Neeraj ordered dinner for them from Sai Sagar Hotel and attended to several other calls, including the nightly call from his mother. It was only in the morning she realized, Maria said, that Neeraj had left his cellphone behind, which was charging in the bedroom. 'I scrolled through the phonebook, found Nishant Lal's number and informed him that Neeraj had left his phone behind.' Neeraj's phone then became the most vital clue in the police investigation.

Emile also later told Inspector Raorane that 'Maria was alone in the flat' when he arrived at Dheeraj Solitaire on the morning of May 7 a little after seven in the morning, adding that he had 'never seen Neeraj Grover'. The first and the only time he had spoken to Neeraj, he said, was when he had called Maria from Kochi, and she had asked him to call on Neeraj's phone as her phone battery was dying. This would be Emile's legal stance right through the trial.

The statements were straightforward. 'But,' said Inspector Raorane, 'it struck me as quite odd that someone like Neeraj, by all accounts a very sociable guy, would leave his phone behind and not even call. He could have done that from anywhere, a friend's cellphone, a public booth. If he had mistakenly left his phone behind he would have definitely called Maria to check.'

On the morning of May 12, six days after Neeraj's disappearance, Inspectors Raorane and Ghosalkar stopped by at Maria's house on their way to work. This was standard practice, he said. 'The last person with whom a missing or dead person has been seen is a natural suspect, that's textbook training.'

Maria's tiny flat was full. Apart from her, Inspector Raorane counted her mother, an aunt, Veronica, and Richard. The actress had summoned her family as soon as Emile left for Kochi on May 9, telling them that the police was harassing her because her friend Neeraj had gone missing. At that point the Malad police had only recorded her and Emile's statements just as they had the statements of the rest of Neeraj's friends. Perhaps the idea of going back alone to the flat where Neeraj had lain dead forty-eight hours ago was unpalatable.

Inspector Raorane, his keen eyes missing nothing, played the mild-mannered cop. 'We were in the flat for about twenty minutes, asking routine questions.' But once the formalities were over there came the pointed questions about the deep gashes on both her palms, and the bruises that had so distracted Kiran earlier when she and Emile had gone to borrow his car. Maria explained away the injuries to her hands saying they were sustained while using a grater to scrape vegetables. 'I thought to myself, if this is what can happen cooking just one meal, how will this girl manage for the rest of her life?'

'And these bruises?' Ghosalkar chipped in. There wasn't a hint of coyness in her response: 'Those are love bites. My fiancé Emile was in town, and we got romantic. . .'

'But you know,' Inspector Raorane said rolling his eyes, 'we are also married people hanh!'

Something was amiss—what exactly he couldn't put a finger on—but he'd been reeled in. 'I was hooked to the case.'

One by one, the officers of Unit IX began calling in Neeraj's friends—Nishant, Deepak Kumar, Haresh—grilling them for hours, and also trying to get a sense of Neeraj's personality. All their stories were of a piece. Police Naik Nandkumar, who was still hunting for Neeraj with Amarnath Grover, told Inspector Raorane, 'He doesn't seem the kind of man who will just go missing. He likes his work, his girlfriends, family, and friends. He belongs too much to this world.'

Nandkumar was sharp, patient, and hard-working, and usually his observations were germane. Inspector Raorane paid heed. 'We were working by elimination. If Neeraj was not the sort to wander off then someone else had to be involved in the case. If so who, and why? I began to concentrate on that.'

Rakesh Maria's instincts, as usual, proved razor sharp. When Neeraj's friends, frustrated by the police's inability to locate him, went to the Crime Branch boss to complain, he confidently pointed a finger at Maria Susairaj. 'You, madam, are my suspect number one.'

'It set them aflutter,' he recalled, smiling at the memory. He repeated his claim a few days later when Maria, this time accompanied by Richard, met him again to ask for permission to leave Mumbai for a while. 'Our parents were anxious back home in Mysore, and our grandfather was ailing,' recalled Richard. 'Give us time, we told him, and we'll come back whenever you need us. But Rakesh Maria just looked at us and said there was no way he could let us leave town as Moni was his prime suspect.'

'How can you say that? What proof do you have against me?' Maria had remonstrated. Rakesh Maria's attention, like the others before him, was arrested by the darkening bruises and gashes on her hands. 'Get a medical done on that Susairaj girl,' he called Unit IX as soon as Maria and Richard walked out of his office. The medical reports indicated that the injuries came from a sharp object like a knife, and not the serrated surface of a vegetable grater.

Amarnath Grover, meanwhile, was becoming tired, anxious, suspicious, and very, very afraid. It had been six days since Ginni had gone missing, and the police had nothing to offer: no clue, no comfort. After some private sleuthing, he arrived at his own deductions. When Inspector Ghosalkar, befriended during the long fruitless search across Mumbai, asked if he suspected anyone of wanting to hurt Neeraj, Amarnath Grover told him of his terrible suspicions about Nishant Lal.

Neeraj was a strapping fellow and of his friends only Nishant Lal was big enough to harm him physically, he said. Also, he was disturbed by the mumbo-jumbo that Nishant had told him the previous day about a tarot card reader whom he had consulted for Neeraj's whereabouts.

'The tarot card reader pulled out a death card and said that Neeraj was tied up somewhere and crying out for help,' he had told Amarnath Grover. Then, seeing the old man overcome with emotion, Nishant had leaned forward and requested him to return to Kanpur. 'The police is doing everything they can and we're here to keep a tab on them. Uncle, please go home and you can come back as soon as there is any information.'

'I find his talk strange,' confided Amarnath Grover, his sense of reason clouded by his anxiety. 'Neeraj is so popular with girls; perhaps Nishant is jealous of that.'

At Ghosalkar's instruction he invited Nishant Lal to Neeraj's flat at Seven Bungalows the next evening where, following a prearranged signal, a team of eight plainclothes policemen grabbed and bundled the young man into a waiting Bolero.

It was to be the only misstep in the entire investigation.

Amarnath Grover was woken up the next morning by a furious Deepak Kumar, who accused him of causing harm to Nishant when all he had done was try to be kind and helpful. The police had detained Nishant through the night, Amarnath Grover realized, with all its attendant implications. 'I am sorry,' he told Deepak. 'But the police asked me for suspects, and I was forced to comply.'

Nishant himself never spoke of it again, and was one of the strongest prosecution witnesses.

~

The morning after Inspector Raorane's visit to her flat, Maria was asked to appear at the Unit IX office in Bandra. It is a smallish space with warren-like rooms, tucked away behind the sprawling police station on a main thoroughfare almost as an afterthought. Maria arrived at 10.30 am 'like a star on a film set', recalled Inspector Raorane, with minders Richard and Veronica in tow. She was directed to a hard wooden bench in the corridor outside and made to wait for the next four hours.

Interrogations are at their heart about power, and the interplay between the interrogator and the interrogated. Physical intimidation is the standard tactic, and employed on poor, petty, or hardened criminals, though after the outcry raised by human rights organizations cops are more careful to camouflage their efforts. For instance, a suspect will be wrapped in a cold towel before he's caned so that there are no visible marks on his person. At other times just a few words delivered with the right amount of menace can suffice. There's the story of a famous encounter cop with a dizzying body count against his name who just had to walk in, cock an eyebrow, and ask, 'Cooper, ya upar?' for the other person to start blabbering. (Cooper is a large municipal hospital in suburban Mumbai.)

But brute intimidation is also unsophisticated and has its limitations, forcing policemen to evolve more refined methods. When he was probing the 1993 blasts Rakesh Maria was known to offer suspects kilos of jalebi, but he'd stop his hospitality at that, refusing them even a drop of water thereafter. Try eating several jalebis without a sip of water to know what exquisite torture that is. 'All this maar-dhaad is outdated,' Inspector Raorane told me. 'You have to read the profile of the person you are questioning and raise yourself to that level.'

After making Maria wait, Inspector Raorane called her in with all the warmth of an apologetic host. She came across as composed, confident, and willing to answer all questions. While Richard and Veronica waited outside, stressed about the elapsing hours, Maria and Inspector Raorane chatted away about her likes and dislikes, her life, her career, her ambitions. He found her rather well read. Like Emile she favoured books on Christianity, and also crime thrillers. He let her move around the room, answer phone calls. 'Her body language suggested over-confidence—she would stroll around the place as if she was in command. At no point did I believe what she said, but I never let it show. It wasn't anything like an interrogation,' said the investigator. Since he had no evidence against her they let her go home. This would become a pattern over the next eight days.

Simultaneously Unit IX and the Malad police began to verify the nature of Maria's relationship with Neeraj, her past, as also her statements to the police. Choreographer Deepak Singh told them how she had come to stay at his house but spent all her nights with Neeraj. The Coffee House Nomads confirmed their public display of intimacy at the party at D'Ultimate, and Neeraj's roommate Haresh Sondarva told the police that Neeraj and Maria slept together. Her ex-boyfriends were scrutinized. Manish was questioned on the phone, Inspector Raorane debated summoning the well-known actor she had been involved with, and called Rakesh Maria for advice. 'Does he have a direct bearing with Neeraj Grover's disappearance?' the senior officer asked.

'At this point I am not sure, sir,' said Raorane.

'In that case, let it be. The media will needlessly get something to chase. Let's instead focus on the other facts of the case.'

'From everything we gathered about her, all that boys' talk about women with dark circles seemed to be true,' Inspector Raorane said grinning snarkily, briefly letting his guard down.

'What about women with dark circles? You mean they should be using eye cream?' I responded flippantly.

'That they are highly sexed.' He seemed genuinely puzzled as I looked at him incredulously. 'Don't you women too have theories about men?'

When it was her turn to be questioned, Nisha Borilkar denied having called Neeraj over to Nishant Lal's place as Maria had claimed in her first statement. She'd spoken to Neeraj on the night of May 6, Nisha admitted, but it was to check his whereabouts and find out how he was doing. She also complained about Emile browbeating her at Malad police station where they had all gone to record their statement on May 8. 'He kept telling me to stop lying and accept that I had called Neeraj over, that I had told him naya maal aaya hai,' she told Inspector Raorane. 'Nothing of the sort had happened.'

Each night, the Unit IX boys got together over dinner to discuss the day's proceedings, relishing the prospects of a complex case. It was to become their daily ritual, analysing, summing up, planning the next day's strategy. They were not entirely sure about Maria's involvement in Neeraj's disappearance, but of the available people she seemed the most promising. It was a game of wearing her down: she would come with Richard and Veronica, be made to wait, sometimes for hours, before being called in for the cat-and-mouse questioning. Only the persistence with which Inspector Raorane questioned her belied his conversational tone, reminding her that this was no drawing room conversation. But while Maria kept her nerve— 'she was a tough cookie,' admitted Rakesh Maria—Richard was beginning to lose his.

'They would call us at nine in the morning, letting us go only past midnight,' he told me, still harrowed by the memory of those nine days. 'They kept asking my sister Roni and I what we knew of Moni's life in Mumbai. I remember getting angry, it was just a missing complaint after all and with what authority were they interrogating us and to this extent!

'The cops kept telling us that if Monica knew something she should reveal it fast and that we should convince her to do so, and we kept asking her why the police was hounding her, but all she kept saying was, "If there was anything, I would have told you." We thought an evil eye had befallen our family and we told ourselves, let us go through this with grace.'

When I told Inspector Raorane what Richard had said about being in the dark, he let out a cynical laugh. 'You believe him, that the family did not know what had happened, hanh?' His trademark 'hanh' conveyed a multitude of emotions.

Inspector Raorane, taking his cue from the Susairaj family's strong Christian ties, changed tack, often leading his discussion with Maria to a religious plane, talking to her about the afterlife and doomsday. 'To be able to speak on all this I must say I am grateful for my education,' he said. 'Daily main use apna cassette sunaata tha.'

'Why do Christians go for confession?' Inspector Raorane would ask Maria. 'So we can go to the Almighty with open hands and hearts. But we're pawns on a chessboard, the Almighty makes us commit things, doesn't he?'

She responded to that with a serene smile. And the last thing he said to her on the night before he let her go, 'Maria, we all have to die and face God, think of yourself as a human being who is a part of God.'

'Good night, sir.'

Lieutenant Vasanth Kumar was in deep trouble. Against his better judgement, he had dropped his roommate Emile to the airport in the middle of the night so he could fly out to Mumbai. Emile had not taken permission to leave the base, and despite Vasanth's repeated pleas had not called his course officer the next day to let him know of his absence. 'Just tell him that I am SIQ [sick in quarantine],' Emile had casually tossed the instruction over his shoulder as he ran into the airport to board the 3.45 am Air India flight 691 to Mumbai. 'You better call him before he asks me, otherwise I'll be jacked,' Vasanth shouted back as the automatic doors to the airport closed on Emile's receding back.

He had tried to make himself invisible in class the next morning, a difficult task in a large room with a handful of men. 'Where's Lieutenant Emile Jerome?' The absence had not escaped course officer Vishal Singh's hawk eye. Vasanth Kumar had no option but to lie. Emile was SIQ, he said.

'With whose permission? Please summon him from the room.'

Vasanth left the classroom and tried to call Emile in Mumbai. His phone was switched off. Bloody hell. It was just past nine on May 7 when he got through to Maria and spoke to Emile. 'You didn't call the course officer as I told you to. He's asking me about you now.'

'Yaar,' Emile was cool, 'I tried to; his phone was unreachable.'

'What are you doing? Please call him now, I told you I'll be jacked otherwise,' Vasanth recalled his words before the police.

But Emile did not call the course officer that day or the next, and Vasanth Kumar was asked to give a written explanation for making a false statement to his superior. An enquiry was initiated into his and Emile's conduct, and an adverse note sent to his personal file. To add to Vasanth's woes Emile's father arrived unexpectedly in Kochi on the evening of May 8 demanding to see his son. Emile should have been back on base that day, but had still not returned. He called to say that he had missed his flight. Vasanth had to spend an entire evening placating Jerome Joseph.

Really, even by navy standards, there were limits to what a course mate could do, Vasanth thought, as he went back into his room on the morning of May 9 only to find Emile sprawled on the bed in his shorts, sleeping like the dead. From that day till the 21st of the month—the day Sub-Inspector Mahesh Tawade reached Kochi to arrest him—Emile displayed no untoward behaviour, said his superiors and course mates. 'If anything he seemed calmer and relaxed,' Vasanth Kumar told the police. 'When I asked him the reason for that, he said, "My problems with my girlfriend have been resolved. I've decided that by year end we will get married, regardless of what my parents have to say."' Back in Mumbai, Maria too was displaying the same steeliness under interrogation.

Emile focused in class and on his swimming, he ate well, and spoke to Maria in hushed tones for long durations, several times a day. Lovebirds! Vasanth Kumar watched Emile, feeling somewhat forlorn as he thought of his own long-distance relationship with his wife. There was just one inexplicable change Vasanth Kumar noticed in his roommate after he returned from Mumbai. Emile had taken to getting up at 4.30 every morning to read the Bible.

After four days of continuous mind games, Maria was beginning to trip up. Inspector Raorane had been using his favourite ploy, one that had served him well during an earlier investigation into the murder of a businessman called Pradeep Jain at Dahisar. His suspect and eventual culprit had been the murdered man's wife's lover. 'I'd call him to my office every day and ask him to help me with the probe. 'What do you think happened?' I kept asking. It was the same with Maria. I asked her to draw up possible scenarios of what could have happened to Neeraj. She kept saying, "I don't know. I know nothing." But if you keep asking the same questions time after time without letting up you may get a clue. The frustration builds up, not just for the interrogator but also for the other person and they can slip up. Pradeep Jain's wife's lover eventually confessed to killing him and even in this case, I began to get a sense that apart from her someone else was also involved in Neeraj's disappearance.'

Like fast bowlers, good investigators too hunt in pairs. Inspector Raorane pulled in his colleague, Sub-Inspector Sagar Shivalkar, into the interrogation sessions. Shivalkar, a tall man with a pleasant, impassive face has the enviable knack for saurian stillness. He could be in a room and be totally unobtrusive. He had a mild-mannered style of questioning, as if he just wanted to hear some stories, but he never missed a note. It also helped that Shivalkar had worked with the Economic Offences Wing, where he had dealt with white-collar suspects. 'Once they [the suspects] secure themselves against a third degree, you can't run a pandu investigation on them, hanh. So how do you overcome that? By being equally intelligent, equally patient, and equally crooked,' said Inspector Raorane, elaborating on Shivalkar's qualities.

Together they played good cop, bad cop with Maria. She had told them that on May 7 she had called up Nishant Lal around noon to tell him that Neeraj had left his phone behind. Later she and Emile had taken a taxi to Dadar at 4–4.30 pm to go shopping and romancing. A basic check on her statement, says Inspector Raorane, threw up many discrepancies.

The first breakthrough in the case came from the phone records, when the police traced the one call that was answered from Neeraj's sister Shikha's phone between 4 and 5 pm on the day he went missing. It was the only one of the hundred and thirty calls that the Grovers had made to Neeraj that day which was answered. The call was traced to Andheri, whereas Maria had said at that time she and Emile were at Dadar. A text message from scriptwriter Sumit Arora to Neeraj, received at 7.36 pm, showed the phone location at Dahisar. Neeraj had commissioned some work from Arora, a freelancer, and he had texted him back to say that the assignment was complete.

'So this was our strategy. I would be sitting and chatting with her, and Sagar would just pop his head into the room to say, a call on Neeraj's phone has been traced to Andheri, and he would leave right after while I would continue talking as before.' Inspector Raorane recounted with relish their efforts to spook Maria into telling the truth. Maria and Emile were actually at Kiran Shreyans's house in Andheri to borrow his car at the time, but she had told the police they were in Dadar. That's why Neeraj's sister's call location had showed up in Andheri.

Maria's second slip-up was when she told the police that she and Emile had travelled to Dadar in a taxi. For Dheeraj Solitaire watchman Satish Kumar Singh distinctly remembered the blue-grey Santro parked in the compound that evening. 'I had just come back from a tea break and I saw a car parked that was not from our building, so I walked up towards it and saw the new tenant in 201 come down with a man, and put two suitcases in the boot of the car. The two of them went up again and returned with a huge plastic bag which they both were holding from the sides and which they struggled to put in the back seat,' he told the police. 'Maria madam saw me watching them and asked me how I was doing as she got into the driver's seat. She then introduced me to the man sitting in the passenger's seat in the front.'

'He's my fiancé,' she told the watchman, caressing Emile's face. Satish Kumar Singh had smiled and saluted smartly as the car drove out of the gates of the building.

'So Maria,' asked Inspector Raorane with endless patience, 'tell me, did you really go shopping with Emile in a taxi to Dadar?' He made sure that as she answered, she could see the watchman being interrogated in the next room from across the window.

'By then I was sure that something drastic had happened to Neeraj. In all these days he had not bothered to get in touch with anyone, and all these lies that we had caught, they had to lead somewhere,' said Inspector Raorane.

'Monu, happy birthday, my darling.'

It was Maria's twenty-eighth birthday on May 17. It had been ten days since Neeraj had gone missing. Had everything been well, she would have celebrated with Neeraj and his friends, as she had told them, or had a rendezvous with Emile, as she had also promised him. But Neeraj's friends had all turned against her after Rakesh Maria's statement, and Emile, her lifeline to sanity, was at the naval base from where he tutored her every day on how to deal with Inspector Raorane's questions. Thrust and parry, both sides planned well.

When she told him about Unit IX questioning the Dheeraj Solitaire watchman Satish Kumar Singh, Emile knew he had to call on his back-up. He had already phoned his friend Jitesh Saini in Mumbai. 'There's a problem, boss, I need your help.'

'Abe teri kitni problems solve karu life mein,' Jitesh had joked, referring to a previous occasion when he had sat up an entire night finishing the drawings for one of Emile's engineering assignments. Both remembered the night well. While he had worked furiously to meet the deadline, Emile had kept him supplied with endless cups of chai made in the room using an immersion rod.

'This is a bit more serious than some drawings. If anyone asks I need you to tell them that Monica and I had borrowed your car on May 7.'

'That's it? Consider it done. But what were you doing in Mumbai?' Emile explained how he had come to Mumbai that day to see Maria without taking prior permission, and for which he was now facing an enquiry.

When she had realized that the watchman in Dheeraj Solitaire was being questioned, Maria changed her statement about the taxi and told Inspector Raorane that they had actually borrowed Emile's friend Jitesh Saini's car on the 7th evening. 'I had forgotten,' she said awkwardly.

She gave the police Jitesh's name and not Kiran's, because Emile was confident that his friend and course mate would weigh in for them, and tell the police whatever they asked him to say. The first inkling Jitesh had of police involvement was when Sub-Inspector Sagar Shivalkar called him to ask about his car. Jitesh bought time by telling him he was busy and that he would revert in a couple of days. On her birthday, soon after he had spoken to her, Emile called Jitesh and gave him Maria's number. 'Yaar, talk to her, she is very troubled, it has something to do with her friend Neeraj Grover going missing, that's why you'll have to say you gave us your car.'

'I don't know why these things are happening to us, we've done nothing,' Maria told Jitesh when he called. Affected by her troubled voice, he promised to deal with the matter and to also meet her the next day to understand why he needed to lie to the police.

Another course mate of Emile's recalled that when he spoke to Maria to wish her on her birthday, she sounded tense and said to him, 'Yaar, please pray for us.'

'I said to her, "C'mon, your good times have just begun. Emile returned from Mumbai the other day and told me that you guys have decided to get married." To which she said, "Arre yaar, there are lots of problems here, tu please pray karva that this year is good for us."'

Like a scorpion stinging itself to death when caught in a circle of fire, Maria had begun to make suicidal errors under pressure. Jitesh Saini told her two irrefutable facts when he came to meet her at home the next day. There was no record, if the Crime Branch were to check, of either her or Emile calling him to borrow his car on the 7th. Second, more pertinently, he did not own a Santro. His car was a Maruti 800. Maria was shattered. She immediately called Emile. Jitesh told another friend, 'I didn't sleep that night wondering what I should be doing, until finally I decided that I could not lie to the police.'

Jitesh also received an unexpected call when he returned to Navy Nagar from Maria's house. It was Maria's brother Richard calling to apologize for all the inconvenience. 'I had no idea that it wasn't your car she used to go out that day. We'll see to it that you do not get into any trouble with the police,' he promised.

The investigation had now taken a more urgent turn. Maria retreated into a shell, talking obsessively only to Emile, and refusing to share anything with her family. Richard felt his judgement cloud. He no longer knew what to believe. The younger sister he thought he knew had turned into a dissembling stranger. 'I was beginning to get worried. I thought she knew something about Neeraj going missing.' Inspector Raorane was no longer the amiable interlocutor they had first met. There was now a rough, contemptuous edge to his talk. 'Maar khayegi kya?' (Would you like to be beaten up?) More than once Richard heard him say this to his sister. Instead of just talking, Raorane had also begun to coax Maria to give her answers in writing, put things on record.

When Inspector Raorane ordered Richard to ensure Maria told them the truth, he could only look at his sister helplessly. 'Pray, Moni, and ask God to give you the strength to remember if you have forgotten something.' The perfect crime lies not in the execution, but in the cover-up. Maria was about to blow hers.

'Sir,' she called Inspector Raorane a couple of days later, 'I'd forgotten that we did not borrow the car from Jitesh

Saini as I mentioned earlier. It slipped my mind but actually I had borrowed it from my friend from Bangalore, Kiran.' After lying about the taxi this was the second time she was changing her account. Suddenly the car had become an important accessory in this mystery.

Maria had already warned Kiran about just such a call, so he was not unduly startled when Sub-Inspector Sagar Shivalkar phoned and asked him to come to the Unit IX office. 'Sure, I said. At about 9.30 pm that night I parked the Santro outside the unit IX office and told my assistants who were travelling with me that I'd be back in fifteen-twenty minutes, and I went in running,' said Kiran.

It was the start of a four-hour ordeal for Kiran. 'They took me to a room, sat me down, and began questioning me. They seemed infinitely patient as compared to my impatience, asking me how I knew Maria, what my relationship with her was, about my car, etc. Then another officer came and asked me exactly the same set of questions, then another and another. I didn't know what was happening and I kept repeating myself. I still couldn't quite connect Maria with what was going on. We are normal people and our friends cannot be criminals.

'That evening, eight policemen asked me the same set of questions, again and again. Your name, father's name, what do you do? And I kept saying, "Sir, is there anything I should be worried about, please tell me what has happened," and they would turn around and say, "Why don't you tell us what happened? She is after all your friend." And when they told me to get the car in the compound, I got really scared. Finally at 1.30 or 1.40 am they said, "You can go home but leave your car behind. Behave with Maria as if you haven't spoken to us at all." But I was so hassled that the minute I got home I called her and told her the Crime Branch guys had called me. "What have you done, Maria?" I asked her. "Did you do anything in my car?" Until this point I had no idea what had happened or even who Neeraj was. She kept saying "Nothing" but sounded very stressed and panicky, and she also told me that she was very scared.'

Forensic examination later yielded blood samples from the back seat that matched Neeraj's sample. By now Inspector Raorane was sure of not just Maria's involvement, but of Emile's as well—he knew that he had been with Maria all through the day Neeraj went missing, and he had been calling her all through the investigation. But Emile was a naval officer—he could not be touched by the civilian police without concrete evidence, so Maria was his only hope. He could see she was at breaking point. The overconfidence had long evaporated, leaving a shrunken wreck of a woman. The dark circles under her eyes seemed accentuated, and there was a nervous tremor in her voice, which had thickened with exhaustion.

When she walked into the Unit IX office the next day, May 20, Maria saw the familiar blue-grey Santro parked in the small compound, and blanched. Inspector Raorane, observing her wan face, decided to play his trump card. She entered the room and as usual put her mobile on the table. He waited for the phone to buzz as he knew it would. It was Emile. As she bent forward to pick it up, he leaned back in his chair. 'Maria, don't answer the phone.'

It was the first time since her interrogation began that he had stopped her from taking calls. They spoke only intermittently after that, both sets of eyes remained trained on the phone that now throbbed every few minutes as Emile grew more and more frantic in Kochi. 'All I did that day was to keep her in the office and not let her answer the phone; I also wanted Emile to get desperate.'

At 10.30 pm Richard, who had been waiting in the corridor of the Unit IX office all day for Maria to emerge, heard his sister cry out loudly. He rushed to see her weeping and Inspector Raorane telling her that he would hit her if she didn't open her mouth. 'He saw me and said, "Just get her to talk," and with that he let us go.' Maria reached home and immediately called Emile. According to Richard, they were on the phone for over an hour.

He had let her go all right, but Inspector Raorane was in a dilemma. He knew that Maria was ready to confess—to what he still didn't know. Could he risk giving her the leeway to talk to Emile and plan further, or should he press home his psychological advantage and get her back again? He debated it with his colleagues over dinner, as it turned out for the final time in this case.

Inspector Raorane took a quick vote: Uske ghar ki apne ghar? (Her house or ours?) Sub-Inspector Shivalkar was of the view that nothing would be lost if they waited till the morning; most others concurred. Then Sub-Inspector Sanjiv Gawade spoke. 'If we are going after her, why not now?' There were no formal charges against Maria, he pointed out. What if she decided to leave town overnight?

It was a tough call for Inspector Raorane. There's a Bombay High Court directive against bringing women suspects to a police station after sunset and before sunrise, though a later amendment in the Criminal Procedure Act allowed for such an arrest in exceptional cases provided they were carried out by a woman officer, after taking permission from a magistrate. Inspector Raorane said of his decision, 'By now I was sure something serious had happened to Neeraj and felt that since we were this close to a confession, we should get her that night itself.'

At 2.30 am a team of six Crime Branch cops, including the required lady police, rang the bell to Maria's flat. Maria's sister Veronica opened the door within seconds. The entire family was awake in the living room. 'I looked at her and said, "Come on Maria, we have to go."'

Richard intervened. 'At this hour? We just got back.' But Inspector Raorane insisted it was urgent. Maria turned to hug her mother and left, accompanied by Richard and Veronica. She broke down as soon as she got into the jeep. 'I heard her tell Roni, Neeraj is no more, Emile killed him and burnt his body,' said Richard, claiming that was the first time he got to know of what had happened. 'My thought was, oh God the inevitable has happened.'

At the Unit IX office, Inspector Raorane offered him a seat inside and told him, 'Don't worry, let her reveal everything, and we will help you.'

'Are you comfortable?' he then asked Maria. His tone had softened now that Maria was ready to confess. 'No,' she couldn't stop crying, eventually bracing herself to start talking. 'As she spoke, my mind went blank, I no longer knew what to believe,' says Richard.

Maria came to Mumbai from Bangalore on April 29, nine days before Neeraj's killing. She had been in Mumbai a month ago, auditioning for a Balaji show. Neeraj Grover, whom she had befriended, had been calling her in Bangalore—television roles, he suggested, were aplenty in Mumbai, and his non-stop banter, laced with delicious double entendres, often reduced her to helpless laughter. After the last few weeks with Emile—his inability to commit, his caginess, and possessiveness—such levity must have been a relief. Neeraj also offered the comfort of the familiar: most men she dated had been from the entertainment industry. It was easy for her to slip into the insidious role-playing—looking into his eyes for that fraction longer, the hint in the smile. It may have been the same for Neeraj, phoning her several times a day, his hand on the small of her back when they met. From such gestures they manufactured intimacy.

But as her first week back in Mumbai went by, there was no word from Balaji Telefilms. The name of the actress who would play Draupadi was also soon announced. Neeraj, who she learnt had been making fun of her diction, was not the all-powerful television mandarin he made himself out to be, and she began to doubt his intentions. She had been seduced, she soon realized. Emile and Neeraj, the two men she was romantically attached to, seemed ironically to mirror their lack of commitment to her. Between them, was she going to remain unmarried, unsuccessful, and unfulfilled?

Call logs show that Emile and Maria spoke twenty-four times on May 6. Lieutenant Vasanth had said that Emile was speaking to Maria 'incessantly'. Emile called her at 11.31 am, 4.30 pm, then again at 6.15, 6.30, 9, 10, and 11.30 pm. Vasanth, who left the room for a party on the naval base at 7.30 pm, recalled Emile talking to Maria as he left.

'At 10.30 when I popped into the room to drink water, I saw Emile pacing in the room, still talking to Maria on the hands-free. As soon as I returned to the room after the party at 11.15 he asked me for the keys to my bike so he could head out to the airport,' Vasanth later told the police. When he protested, Emile told him, 'Yeh meri life ka maamla hain' (It's a matter of my life). He was trembling and distraught as he said this. 'Earlier too Maria had pressured Emile for marriage so I said, "Speak to her again, get her to see sense," and he said, "This time she is serious."'

It was too late for afterthoughts, Emile added, as he had already booked his ticket. 'She is psychologically down and I need to be there, I'll come back and face the consequences,' he said urgently. Their course mate and neighbour, Lieutenant Ajay Sham Pandey, who had been dining out in town that evening, told the police that he got a telephone call from Emile at around 9 pm asking for the PIN number to his VISA credit card. The police in their charge sheet quote Pandey as saying, 'I said I'd give it to him but he should not write it down anywhere, and even if he did, to tear the paper right after he had used the PIN number. I did not feel the need to ask him why he needed it.' Emile used Pandey's credit card to book a seat online for the next morning's Air India Flight 691, which left Kochi for Mumbai at 3.45 am.

What is crucial is the timing of Emile's call to Pandey. He called him at about 9 pm, almost half an hour before Maria had interrupted Neeraj's dinner, insisting that he come over to her house to help her shift. Telephone records from that evening show she had called Neeraj at 9.28 pm and then again at 9.55 pm.

Had she and Emile already planned something, as the prosecution alleged, or was it, as Emile later told Vasanth, that he had to go to Mumbai because Maria had given him an ultimatum? If Emile did not make up his mind about marrying her, he would have to choose once and for all between her and his parents. Then why, when she knew that Emile would arrive the next morning, did Maria invite Neeraj over? This mystery was at the unfathomable core of the events that followed.

Maria told the police that when she spoke to Emile at around 11.30 pm on the night before Neeraj died, she had also told him that Neeraj was 'acting funny' with her that day. 'Emile then asked me whether he should come down and I said, no, he will be leaving after dinner.' Again, the statement did not match the facts. Emile had already booked his ticket to Mumbai by then. Was she not aware that he was coming over? And if he was 'acting funny' why did she let Neeraj stay the night?

None of her distress was reflected in Maria's behaviour with Neeraj that night. After he reached her flat, Neeraj spoke to his mother who said he sounded his usual happy self. He also spoke to his friends Barsha and Nisha, not saying anything untoward about Maria's state of mind to either of them. In fact, he put the phone on speaker mode and made Nisha speak to Maria, who promised to throw a party for her birthday on the 17th.

In between he had also briefly spoken to Emile who called on his number at 11.41 pm and then again at 11.55 pm. This, Emile told the police, was on account of Maria's phone battery running out.

The Air India flight was on schedule. By 6.30 am, Emile was out of the airport and on his way to Maria's home in an autorickshaw. En route he called Neeraj's phone. He did so, he told the police, because he was not sure of the way and he couldn't get through to Maria's phone. But this was not his first visit to the building. He had spent a night at Maria's neighbour Mayuri Prajapati's flat in Dheeraj Solitaire just five months ago, when he had come to see Maria off to the UK.

Was he calling to confirm his suspicions about Neeraj and Maria? Because he disbelieved her when she had told him that Neeraj would leave after dinner? When he went back to the naval base, Emile told Vasanth that he'd felt insecure about Neeraj's presence in Maria's life.

We know what happened next only through Maria's recorded confession to the magistrate, not through Emile's version of events. In her confession Maria said that her doorbell rang some minutes past seven that morning, and when she opened the door she found Emile standing there, a knapsack on his back. Without saying a word he walked straight into the bedroom where he found Neeraj fast asleep and in his underpants. When Neeraj opened his eyes he looked at Emile, and then at Maria. 'Oh, so this is your boyfriend,' he said. Provoked, Emile began raining blows on Neeraj. As both men grappled with each other, Maria said she tried to intervene but could control neither.

'They pushed me, I fell down and by the time I got up I saw Emile had stabbed Neeraj with a knife he'd got from my kitchen. I tried to hold the knife and stop him and thereby sustained injuries to my palm. But Emile pushed me again, and stabbed Neeraj once more who fell down. I then saw Emile kicking him. I was screaming but Emile turned to me and shut my mouth, threatening to kill me also.'

Dheeraj Solitaire is one of those faux-modern multi-storeyed constructions that make up so much of the landscape of North Mumbai. The façade is posh, with a large lobby and elevators, but the bulk of the space is taken up for these appearances. The apartments that so fascinated Ram Gopal Varma are matchbox-sized themselves, with thin walls and grille windows, piled next to one another, offering little privacy. But Dipak Sherawat, whose flat is in the building right opposite Maria's, separated by an alley ('We can look into their bedroom, their hall, and their kitchen') recalled waking up at his usual time of seven on the morning of May 7. He and his flatmate Divyaprakash came into the living room, where they read the newspapers till 8.30 but during this time neither man heard any screaming.

Police investigations suggested that within minutes of Emile's arrival at the flat Neeraj lay dead on the floor. His blood had turned the small bedroom into a soggy mess, soaking the couple too. Emile and Maria stared at one another and in the onrush of emotion drew close. But then Emile stepped forward and hit her, and even as the blood around them congealed, he forced her to have sex with him. After which Maria said she went to have a bath to wash off the stains, leaving Emile in the room with Neeraj's body. But the sight of his dead adversary spreadeagled on the floor played havoc with Emile. He banged on the bathroom door, and as Maria unlatched it, he pushed his way in and they had sex again.

She called it rape. Tactical, was Rakesh Maria's verdict. 'It was a way of cementing an unspoken deal. They were in this together now.'

For the next three hours, they washed and mopped, pulled off the mattress covers, the bedsheet, the pillow-cases, the rose-coloured curtains that Maria had purchased the previous evening from Hypercity mall with her neighbour Mayuri, and which had just acquired a darker hue. Together they stripped the room of everything that showed any signs of a bloodstain. And yet, for all the care they took, they missed the outer latch of the bedroom, the specks on the television speaker, the discoloration on Maria's jeans with the label Skinny stitched on the inside.

In the midst of all this, Emile answered Vasanth's call wanting to know why he had still not spoken to their course officer. 'Yaar, I tried, his phone was unavailable,' he fobbed off his roommate, working around the flat with military precision, already thinking ahead as he upturned Maria's suitcases on the floor.

He instructed her to go get a carving knife, a fresh set of curtains, a large duffel bag, and a room freshener as he dragged Neeraj's body into the bathroom.

But before she went out shopping Emile wanted Maria to call up one of Neeraj's friends and tell them that Neeraj had left her house at 1.30 am and that he had forgotten his phone. 'Tell them that they should come and get it from here at night.' Maria found Nishant Lal's number and called him.

The appropriately named Hypercity mall, with its gleaming chrome and steel walls, and young patrons—men and women fresh off some call centre shift—was fifteen minutes away from Dheeraj Solitaire. On a weekday afternoon like May 7, one could get there in under ten minutes. A police chowki fell on the way, which Maria ignored as her autorickshaw rattled past.

'All the while I was out of the house, Emile was on the phone with me,' she told the magistrate in her confession.

Vivek Tiwari, one of the cashiers, recalled Maria coming to his kiosk at about noon that day with a double bedsheet and a comb. 'She gave me her HSBC debit card, but as I was totalling the bill she changed her mind about buying the comb. I cancelled Rs 49, tallied her signature and asked her why there was no photograph affixed on her debit card.' He remembered looking carefully at her face before scanning the card.

Vaishali More, working on cash counter number 14 on May 7, recollects Maria for quite different reasons. Maria reached More's counter with another bill of Rs 1,776, for which she wanted to pay in cash. Was it so that there would be no account of these purchases? The bill was for a travel bag, a large bread knife, room freshener, and rose-coloured curtains identical to the ones she had bought the previous evening. She gave the cashier Rs 2,000. 'Do you have six rupees in change? I asked her,' recalled More to the police, 'but she suddenly lost her cool over the non-availability of change.'

'What's the point of running such a large mall if you do not make small change available. I have no change, if you want to give me the money, give it, else keep it,' Maria said in a raised voice. 'I took the money from one of my colleagues and gave it to her after which she left the mall.'

This small, irrational outburst was the only sign of strain Maria showed throughout that day. Vishal Vijay, a television actor who was an acquaintance of Neeraj's, had just finished checking his email at Cyber Masti on Malad Link Road and was going home when he spotted Maria on the other side of the road. They had met at the party at D'Ultimate. She was sitting in an autorickshaw surrounded by large Hypercity bags. 'Hell-lo!' Maria beamed at him as they exchanged pleasantries from their respective autos. She told him she had just rented a place close by, and as the three-wheeler moved ahead, she leaned out and chimed, 'We should meet up sometime.'

When she got home Neeraj's body was already in the bathroom. Emile had emptied her two suitcases and also lined up the large plastic bags in which she had purchased stuff for the house the previous evening. 'Do any of your friends have a car we can borrow?' He told her he had already tried Jitesh's number but it was unavailable. Jitesh was then serving on a ship where there was no mobile network.

Maria remembered her meeting with Kiran at her choreographer friend Deepak Singh's house; he had a car. Kiran was frosty and unwilling but Maria, in desperation, cast all dignity aside and began to plead. 'Kiran, please please please please. . .'

'Emile had in the meantime unpacked the large knife she had bought. Then he asked her to clean up the living room, and as he disappeared into the bathroom, knife in hand, he gave her the final instruction: 'Do not come in.'

The weight of human life, prana, is said to be a mere twenty-one grams, but the human body with its joints and muscle, bone and tissue is a far hardier thing. It took Emile three hours and every ounce of his formidable strength to cut up Neeraj's body; not into three hundred pieces as was sensationally reported, but into a more scientific dismembering at the joints: the head, the torso, the elbow joints, the joints at the knees, the ankles.

After this Herculean exertion Emile and Maria cleaned themselves up and set out for Kiran's house to fetch his car just short of 4 pm. But before that Maria dropped in at Mayuri Prajapati's flat, 203-B.

The previous evening the two women had gone shopping at Hypercity where, over a sandwich in the food court, Maria had told her about her friend Neeraj Grover who was going to get her a role in a television serial. Later the same night Maria had used Mayuri's facilities for a bath, since her own bathrooms were still dirty. As she had stepped out, Neeraj whom she had called over, emerged from the lift. Maria introduced Mayuri to Neeraj, just as she later did Emile. 'You remember him, don't you? My fiancé. . .' Emile had smiled shyly as Maria and Mayuri spoke briefly. Maria then told Mayuri that they were going out on a date, and the two walked away, hand in hand.

Unknown to Mayuri, they were back soon after from Kiran's house with his blue-grey Santro. The luggage was packed. Two suitcases and three large plastic bags which carried Neeraj, his clothes, the curtains, the mattress cover, and everything in the room that had been bloodied and was disposable. They took three turns carrying it all down, both of them holding the final bag from either side only to find the watchman Satish Kumar Singh standing by the car and looking curious. Maria was the first to recover her poise. 'Kaise ho?' she smiled, sliding into the driver's seat as she caressed Emile's cheek, before introducing him to the security guard.

Then they drove out of the gates of Dheeraj Solitaire.

It was 6 am. Maria had been talking to the police for over three hours continuously, sparing no detail for her spellbound audience. Inspector Raorane, exhausted but exhilarated, had one concern now. They needed to recover the body. Without a body there would be no case, no conviction.

'Maria,' he said encouragingly, 'can you show us where you took Neeraj's body?'

She nodded tiredly.

'Are you ready?' He wasn't just referring to the trip ahead. By now she understood him well. 'Yes, I know the consequences are harsh.'

Half an hour later, said Richard, they left the Unit IX office at Bandra. 'The police kept me back in the Unit IX office saying I'd have to stay put till they all returned.' On his way, Inspector Raorane picked up Inspector Nalawade and the others from the Malad police station. Their destination was the picnic spot of Manor, 92 kilometres north of Mumbai.

While they were posted at INS Shivaji, Lonavla, Emile and his batchmates sometimes went for picnics to Bordi, a sylvan spot close to Manor. 'That's where we will go now,' he had told Maria. But before that he had a couple of errands to run. Within minutes of their leaving Dheeraj Solitaire he made Maria pull up on Link Road, not far from the Parkar petrol pump. The attendant there, Vinod Kumar Mishra (who later identified Emile in jail), said, 'He came to the petrol pump between 5.30 and 6 pm carrying a yellow-coloured five-litre Saffola Losorb jerry can and said his car, parked on Malad Link Road, had run out of petrol. "My wife is in the car and I really need the petrol," he said.' When Mishra told him they were not allowed to sell loose fuel, Emile brought out his identification card. 'I am an officer with the Indian navy and a responsible man,' he said. 'Please help me.'

'The ID card convinced me of his intentions and I decided to sell him petrol worth Rs 250,' said Mishra. Later, much further north, they stopped again at the paan-beedi stall of Amar Bahadur Yadav to buy a lighter. It was nearly 7 pm and twilight had fallen. 'I remember him because I had only one lighter left in my shop which I couldn't locate and this man was getting impatient. 'Jaldi karo,' he kept saying. Yadav eventually found the lighter and sold it to Emile for five rupees.

Beyond Borivali, the suburbs get shabbier, dirtier, the refuse of Mumbai lining their streets. The high-rises give way to unpainted three-storey dumps, and most doctors' degrees here read not MBBS, but the non-allopathic BHMS. This world is captured in beautiful detail in the urban landscapes of the artist Sudhir Patwardhan.

Unlike Oshiwara, bulldozing its way into a shinier, brassier newness, the battle with modernity seems to be lost here, except for some feeble defence provided by wayside motels—there's Hotel Haveli advertising Raw: The Disc, and Hotel Hollywood, and the Vegas Hotel. But cross the detritus of urban India at the toll naka—it was for fear of the cameras installed here which capture all passing vehicles that Maria had initially lied to the police about her and Emile travelling in a taxi—and the beauty of the landscape begins to reveal itself. All around are thickly carpeted hills, the verdure of summer, and the cool waters of the Surya river. The police team could have almost fooled themselves into believing they were headed out for a picnic.

They drove 85 kilometres straight up until the junction called Ten Naka without mishap, but as they took the right turn next to the Manor police station on the Wada-Kalyan highway, Maria seemed to lose her bearings. 'We took a small left somewhere here.' But where, she could not locate. The police team drove down that road three times with no success. 'We were sleepless, exhausted, and I thought she was pulling a number,' said Inspector Raorane. At one point he stopped both the cars, got down, and roared at Maria, threatening her with dire consequences. 'But then Veronica came to me and said, "I know my sister really well, she is not lying, she really can't remember, give her some time and she'll find the right spot,'" said Inspector Raorane.

Maria stayed put there, thought hard for a while and then asked the driver to go back to the turn from Manor police station. 'From here drive at 60 kmph,' she instructed. After ten minutes she ordered the driver to stop. On the left was a small kachcha path going in. The paddy fields all around had been set on fire—for the next season's crop—and there, next to some bushes, under a large tree, she pointed the police team to a heap of bones which lay there, plain for anyone to see.

'I was really surprised to see the place, it was almost as if it was there for the explicit purpose of disposing of a body,' recalled Inspector Raorane. In utter silence, broken only by the whistling sound of the truck tyres hitting macadam on the far-off highway, they looked at the half-burnt remains of Neeraj Grover. The skull lay some ten feet away from the ribcage. As they scrounged around they discovered bones, incinerated clothes, a chain with a locket, the soot and the ash.

Inspector Nalawade called Unit IX senior inspector Ashok Borkar, who in turn called Rakesh Maria to let him know that the missing boy's case had finally been solved. Within hours, a fortnight after Neeraj Grover's disappearance, the Crime Branch boss was on national television hosting a press conference and giving out the sensational details of Neeraj Grover's killing.

What did it feel like seeing Neeraj's remains, I asked Inspector Raorane. 'Relief. I thought finally I can go back home and get some sleep.'

The team returned to Mumbai at 8 pm. Two weeks ago, Maria and Emile had returned to Mumbai from Manor at about the same time. The first thing the couple had done was stop at a mattress shop. Kamlesh Jain, proprietor of the Sunshine Foam Furnishing shop, recalled Maria coming into his shop and asking him to send two of his workers to pick up two mattresses from her flat which were in urgent need of fresh covers.

Then she called up a painter, Dhiraj Kumar Shukla, asking him to send his men to her flat the next morning as she needed to get the flat painted immediately. When the painters arrived at flat 201-B in the morning, Maria, disregarding their advice to start work first on the living room, told them to paint the bedroom. 'And it needs to be done by today itself,' she instructed, leading them inside. Shukla said he was taken aback by the ugly blackish stains all over the wall near the bathroom. 'What happened here?' he asked wonderingly.

'They've been there since before we moved in,' Maria responded shortly. She gave him Rs 2,000 as an advance, insisting once again that the bedroom had to be painted in a day. But as soon as the bedroom and the passageway were painted, she called him to say she had changed her mind about the rest of the house.

As soon as Maria had finished her harrowing narration at the Unit IX office, Inspector Raorane asked Assistant Inspector Mahesh Tawade to go to Kochi to arrest Emile.

Vasanth Kumar said he had no idea anything was amiss until he went into his room after class and found Emile sitting there. He had been detained there by the naval authorities.

'What are you doing here in the room?' Vasanth asked.

'Yaar, it's about Maria's friend Neeraj Grover, he can't be traced and Monica is not reachable. I had gone with her to register the missing complaint, and now the police is here to take me to Mumbai and question me in that regard.'

'That same guy who is a druggie and who sleeps around?' Vasanth now recalled Emile returning from Mumbai and telling him about Maria's missing friend. This is what Emile had told him, further perpetuating his and Maria's story about Neeraj being into drugs: 'Neeraj had gone to her house on the 6th on the pretext of helping her but when one of his friends called him to say, "naya maal aaya hai," he left immediately and has been missing since.'

It was only when he got a call from one of his superiors later that night asking him to separate all of his roommate's things and make an inventory of them, that the full horror of what had happened hit Vasanth. 'Why an inventory, sir?'

'Why? Have you not been seeing TV?'

Vasanth then switched on the television, tuning in to *Sansani* on Aaj Tak. On the same programme which had given him and Emile so many hours of amusement, he saw the report of Neeraj's death, and Rakesh Maria, with a row of cops standing proudly behind him, giving the gruesome details of the killing. On a split screen Vasanth saw Maria in a black salwar kameez, her face covered by her dupatta, surrounded by cops, trying to evade the cameras she had so avidly sought all through her adult life.

In Kochi, the body receipt (military terminology for handing over a suspect) from the naval authorities took longer than expected. As a result Assistant Inspector Tawade and Emile missed their flight to Mumbai. All through the journey Emile maintained a stoic silence. 'I am an officer with the Indian navy,' he kept reminding his civilian captor.

In the Crime Branch lock-up, he pleaded with Inspector Raorane to let him meet Maria 'just once'.

'He was sure that Maria would never, ever betray him,' said Inspector Raorane. "Whatever Monu has told you is the truth. I have nothing more to add to that," he said.'

Unknown to him, on May 27 Maria had gone to court and recorded a detailed confession before a magistrate in which she blamed Emile for killing Neeraj, hacking up his body, disposing of it in the jungles of Manor, and of also raping her twice. This could, unlike her police confession of six days ago, be used in court.

Inspector Raorane did not tell Emile that Maria had accused him of murder and rape. Emile was to discover this several weeks later, when the charge sheet was filed. In the meantime he helped them recover the two knives with which Neeraj was stabbed, hidden in the drain of one of the bathrooms of Maria's flat, and the bread knife with which the body was cut, buried some distance away from Neeraj's remains.

Inspector Raorane later remembered meeting Emile in the sessions court as soon as the murder trial began. He walked up to him and said, 'In life you must know whom to trust and how much.'

'I know, sir,' Emile looked him in the eye. 'I have learnt it the hard way.'

But the following year, on October 26, 2009, Emile and Inspector Raorane had another encounter which he reported to both Rakesh Maria and the trial court. That day Emile, evading the police constables accompanying him, walked up to the investigating officer and said, 'Why are you pursuing this case? Am I some Chhota Rajan or Dawood Ibrahim that you need to follow up on this case so insistently?'

'Whatever you wish to say, tell it to the court,' the stunned officer told Emile.

'That I will, but I will also see you; it's not like I am going to be behind bars for my whole life.'

EPILOGUE

ON JUNE 30, 2011, three years and twenty-three days after Neeraj Grover was killed and his body hacked to pieces, the trial court convicted Emile Jerome and Maria Susairaj.

Judge M.W. Chandwani began to read his judgment aloud. The courtroom was densely packed with reporters, with not even standing room on offer. In the dock, the tension was suffocating as former lovers Maria and Emile refused to look at one another.

An audible gasp went around the courtroom as the judge exonerated Maria Susairaj of the charge of murdering Neeraj Grover. Relying extensively on her confession—the only account we have of what transpired on the morning of Neeraj's death—Maria was convicted of destruction of evidence, and sentenced to three years' imprisonment.

It had taken a little over that long for the trial to conclude, and Maria had already finished her term. She could walk out of jail the next morning—which she did amidst unprecedented media frenzy in Mumbai.

On her first evening out of jail in three years, Maria chose to hold a press conference. She would not talk about her confession or entertain questions about her relationship with either Neeraj or Emile, her lawyer stipulated. In the full heat of the media's glare, he then whipped out a photograph of the dismembered remains of Neeraj Grover found at Manor.

'Mr Umesh Kumawat,' he directly addressed the reporter who had first run the story of Neeraj's body being hacked into three hundred pieces. 'Where are the three hundred pieces? I can see only five or six,' he said before handing over the photograph to whoever cared to count, while Maria shuddered delicately.

If he was seeking relief for his client from public opprobrium, it wasn't forthcoming. Neeraj Grover's friends, incensed by this travesty, walked in to disrupt the press conference, shouting their protest. In the mêlée that followed, Maria was escorted out, held protectively by her brother and lawyers, while the media trampled over one another to chase her for photographs and sound bytes.

It was great theatre for the actress manqué—only this time she occupied centre-stage.

Emile Jerome was convicted of 'culpable homicide not amounting to murder', and sentenced to ten years' imprisonment. Citing Exception 1 of Section 300 of the Indian Penal Code, Judge Chandwani read out: 'Culpable homicide is not amounting to murder if the offender, whilst deprived of the power of self-control by grave and sudden provocation, causes the death of the person who gave provocation.'

While Maria Susairaj walked free, Emile Jerome went back to Taloja jail, on the outskirts of Mumbai, where he is Qaidi no C-31.

Emile's stint in jail so far has been a fraught one. He got into demonstrative scraps with the authorities at Arthur Road jail, where he was first lodged as an undertial. He complained of assault and that he had been denied basic amenities. When he came to court for his trial, he often spoke to reporters about the pathetic prison conditions. In turn, jail officers charged Emile with unruly behaviour. When he protested about being shifted from the barracks he shared with, among others, the gangster Abu Salem, they moved him to another jail on the outskirts of Mumbai. There he was put in charge of a teaching programme to train his illiterate fellow prisoners. His minor rebellions effectively subdued, gaolers now describe him as a model prisoner.

Acknowledgements

I OWE AN enormous debt to all my colleagues at *Mumbai Mirror* for their indulgence, resourcefulness, and assistance.

Grateful thanks also to Ramananda Sreenivas and Nagaraja Dixit for making the trip to Mysore so memorable.

Saira Menezes, Namita Devidayal, Aakar Patel, and Bachi Karkaria for their generous friendship and encouragement.

Priya Gupta who can, and did move mountains.

My dearest friend and first reader, Tushita Patel, whose affections and unfailingly crisp advice have seen me though the years; her friendship is most cherished.

My brother Aditya whose sense of humour and equanimity keep the peace at our home.

The idea for this book started with a phone call one afternoon from Chiki Sarkar. She has since nurtured it with her sharp instincts, kindness, and enormous belief. Without her persuasion, gentle or otherwise, this book would have never been written.

My publisher and editor, Meru Gokhale, whose meticulous eye has made this a sharper book. Thanks for the attention and care with which she has seen this book out into the world.

An endeavour like this depends entirely on the cooperation of the people interviewed. A great many of them gave generously of their time, often trusting me with their personal histories. To everyone I have spoken to for the book, on or off the record, my profound gratitude.

A Note on the Author

Meenal Baghel, editor of Mumbai's leading newspaper, *Mumbai Mirror*, uncovers the true story of one of the most sensational crimes to hit the maximum city in recent years. Using exclusive interviews with the police, the friends and families of the victim and the accused, Baghel draws a riveting picture of a death whose mystery has not faded, even though the killers may have been found. Gripping and hard-hitting, *Death in Mumbai* is a fascinating insight into a new type of crime affecting the Indian city.